£6.75

Big Issues

Ann Cartwright

Published by Heinemann Educational Publishers
Halley Court, Jordan Hill, Oxford OX2 8EJ
A division of Reed Educational and Professional Publishing Ltd

OXFORD MELBOURNE AUCKLAND
JOHANNESBURG BLANTYRE GABORONE
IBADAN PORTSMOUTH (NH) USA CHICAGO

06 05 04 03 02
10 9 8 7 6 5 4 3 2 1

ISBN 0 435 23335 1

Cover design by Miller, Craig and Cocking
Typeset by 𝍏 Tek-Art, Croydon, Surrey
Printed and bound in the United Kingdom by
Clays Ltd, St Ives plc

Tel: 01865 888058 www.heinemann.co.uk

Contents

Introduction

The Programme of Study for Citizenship at Key Stage 3 sets out specific areas of study to help students' Knowledge and Understanding about becoming Informed Citizens (KUIC). These include students being taught about:

a) the legal and human rights and responsibilities underpinning society, basic aspects of the criminal justice system, and how both relate to young people

b) the diversity of national, regional, religious and ethnic identities in the United Kingdom and the need for mutual respect and understanding

c) central and local government, the public services they offer and how they are financed, and the opportunities to contribute

d) the key characteristics of parliamentary and other forms of government

e) the electoral system and the importance of voting

f) the work of community-based, national and international voluntary groups

g) the importance of resolving conflict fairly

h) the significance of the media in society

i) the world as a global community, and the political, economic, environmental and social implications of this, and the role of the European Union, the Commonwealth and the United Nations.

In writing this collection of Drama scripts, I hope to engage pupil interest in these concepts of Citizenship. Issues of respect, tolerance and human rights have always been part of pupil study. The word 'Citizenship' merely provides a focus.

Citizenship covers all aspects of social interaction. Some of the issues covered by these scripts and sketches are of a sensitive nature. Therefore, I would recommend that teachers use their professional judgement in selecting which scripts to read with their classes.

I hope that both teachers and pupils enjoy this collection and that the issues raised will be thought-provoking, providing stimulus for further personal investigation.

Ann Cartwright

Section 1:
Confidence and Responsibility
Scripts for the Mind

Budget

List of Characters

Dad
Mum
Tina
Gavin
Sophie

A family meeting.

DAD   Right. I think you know why I have called this family meeting.

TINA   I think that it is not my fault if Sophie is such a slob and leaves everything lying around all over the place.

SOPHIE   What? Excuse me!

TINA   I have repeatedly asked for my own room and been denied my request.

DAD   Tina . . .

TINA   I refuse to take sole responsibility and grounding punishment for the state of our room.

DAD   Thanks for the opinion, but that heap of wreckage you two laughingly call your room is not why I called this meeting.

GAVIN   Dad, don't you think that Tina is totally and insanely paranoid these days and should be put in a home?

SOPHIE   Yeah. A dogs' home.

TINA   Yeah, right. Gang up on me, why don't you? I don't care.

DAD   Excellent. Good start to the meeting. The actual reason I called this meeting is because of the family holiday we are taking this summer.

SOPHIE	To the villa in Spain!
GAVIN	Instead of last year's poky hotel room in Spain.
TINA	With dripping taps. A deliberate decision to drive us mad. And they couldn't take the 'flea-ridden dump' criticism. I mean, hello? Problem or what?
GAVIN	Could somebody pull her batteries out, please?
TINA	Could somebody stamp on Gavin, please?
DAD	If we are having this holiday in Spain, this very *expensive* holiday in Spain, then we are going to have to *budget*.
TINA	Gavin thinks that's something to do with a squawky little bird.
GAVIN	(*to Tina*) You're a squawky little bird.
MUM	(*entering*) Dashed off my feet, I am. Gavin, cup of tea for your mother.
GAVIN	I did it yesterday when you came in from work!
MUM	Now.
GAVIN	(*getting up and making tea*) It's under protest.
MUM	I do not have a problem with that. (*Sits at table with the rest.*) Good evening, family. How is my little brood?
DAD	I'm just telling them about how we've got to budget to be able to afford the villa in Spain.
MUM	True. Is that as far as you've got? I didn't miss anything else?
DAD	No. I am just about to tell them *how* we are going to budget.
SOPHIE	I don't like that emphasis on the word 'how'. Do you, Tina?
TINA	It sounds as if it is something we will not like.
MUM	You will *not* like it, Tina. You are quite right. We never do anything in this family that you children will like, you know that. (*To Dad*) Tell them, Beloved.

DAD	We're going to stop *buying* things!
MUM	Easy, isn't it? (*Gavin gives her tea.*) Is this for me? How sweet of you to do that without having your arm twisted up behind your back.
GAVIN	(*sitting back down*) I take it the stop-buying remark was aimed solely at us, right?
DAD	No, no, no. Your mum and I will be budgeting as well. It's just that it will affect you three more, as it is you three who bring the most pointlessly expensive garbage into this house.
SOPHIE	I see. And I'll bet you've made a list, haven't you?
MUM	We certainly have. Now then, no more rubbish can come into this house. Not even a little bit. Fashion, my chicks, is dead.
DAD	When all the other young people are buying the latest media-hyped craze, you will not be.
MUM	You will be saving your pennies and putting them into your piggy-banks for the holiday, when you can then do splishy-splashy in the villa's private swimming pool. Won't that be so much nicer than a silly old pair of jeans that you don't really want in the first place? Hm?
SOPHIE	May I say . . .
DAD	The Chair recognises Sophie.
SOPHIE	Thank you. May I say that I do not bring rubbish into this house. I am certainly not influenced by the media. I make my own choices. I only buy what I need.
DAD	(*controlling himself*) Sophie, pet, you are wearing a hat with a tiger's head and paws on the front of it.
SOPHIE	This is high fashion. Everyone's wearing them. Haven't you seen the ads on the telly? I'm not going to be left out.

GAVIN	Fashion victim. Controlled by the media. It's sad really.
MUM	How much did you pay for it?
SOPHIE	Can't remember.
GAVIN	£10.99.
SOPHIE	That's a lie!
GAVIN	I was with you when you bought it!
SOPHIE	Oh, yes! That was the day you bought the new trainers. The top fashion ones with the sound effects in the soles. You know. The ones you don't wear any more because all your mates were laughing at you. How much were they now, Gavin? Two quid? Three quid? Surely not more?
GAVIN	Can't remember.
TINA	Fifty quid! At least! Squandering money!
GAVIN	Ah, but they were essential. I couldn't go around barefoot, could I?
SOPHIE	You don't wear them at all! They're at the back of your wardrobe with the dust and the spiders.
GAVIN	Well, how was I to know that fashions would change that fast? And anyway, who begged for a micro-scooter then and never uses it now?
TINA	I . . . don't remember . . . doing that . . .
GAVIN	A poor and feeble attempt to lie your way out of having been guilty of being manipulated by the media. An executive office-toy. And where do you use it? In the kitchen! Sad person!
MUM	Wait a sec. I'm writing all this down. £10.99 . . . £50 . . . £25 . . .
DAD	Then we have the two main drains on resources. Firstly, games. Sophie and Gavin – beserk buyers and demanders of Game Boy stuff and CD Roms. They

	announce it – you buy it. Forever keeping up with your friends.
MUM	I'm fed up of seeing you squatting over that Game Boy thing. Every time I walk into the room, you're staring intently at your knees or waggling that handset around. Not only is it expensive – frankly, I think it's weird.
GAVIN	It's the modern entertainment!
SOPHIE	Everybody does it!
MUM	At about £30 a time? More if it's one of the latest games!
DAD	It's too expensive! Get your Scrabble out!
MUM	I won't even begin on the second resource drain: mobile phones!
TINA	Phones are essential.
GAVIN	We need them for safety.
SOPHIE	You can't take them off us.
MUM	I agree. But you don't have to update them any more.
TINA GAVIN SOPHIE	But – !
MUM	Phones are for talking into. You lot wear them like FBI badges for some hi-tech credibility. All you do is play games on them and text message your friends about I-love-you and see-you-at-the-Pizza-Palace! You buy covers for them, update them, then chuck the old ones away! You chuck *telephones* away!
DAD	I remember when we first had a telephone in our house when I was a child.
SOPHIE	Here we go.
DAD	We stood round it in awe and wonderment at its miraculous abilities. Awe and wonderment. Now – they're disposable! What is the world coming to?

TINA	If we could . . .
MUM	(*writing it down*) Ninety quid multiplied by three . . .
TINA	If we could get back to the present for a moment, please.
GAVIN	And refocus this meeting on the *entire* family and not just the kids.
SOPHIE	Then we would see that there are further savings to be made via the *parents*.
DAD	Good point. Your mother and I have decided to go out less for the next few months.
MUM	Should save a couple of quid. (*Jots it down.*) There. Any questions?
SOPHIE	Yes. What about the rubbish you buy?
DAD	Rubbish?
MUM	What rubbish?
TINA	The endless collection of braces and ties.
DAD	They're very business-like. They're power-dressing for work.
GAVIN	Twenty sets of them? And shoes! Millions of them. It's like living with an executive centipede.
SOPHIE	And the car-boot sale obsession. One flyer and you're off.
MUM	I get some very good bargains. It's saving money. And – and it's for the family.
TINA	Mum, the family doesn't need any more scatter-cushions, throws or funny-looking candles, thank you.
GAVIN	Then there was the sandwich-maker.
DAD	I needed one.
TINA	The bread-maker.
MUM	I needed one.
SOPHIE	The facial sauna!

DAD	I needed one!
GAVIN	Then why are all these things stuffed in the kitchen sink cupboard?
MUM	Storage. I intend to re-arrange them after.
SOPHIE	After what?
TINA	Exactly. Surplus to requirements.
GAVIN	Shop windows, catalogues, advertisements, telly, radio . . . We just can't resist. We are *all* victims of the media.
SOPHIE	And we *all* have to budget.
MUM	Kids can be so . . .
DAD	Smug.
MUM **DAD**	Exactly.

Democracy

List of Characters

Pleb 1

Pleb 2

PFP 1

PFP 2

BEU 1

BEU 2

Dick Tator

A street. Two election platforms are side by side with walking distance between them. Plebs walk between them, reading leaflets from various political parties.

PLEB 1 Hmm. Those speeches were quite interesting. Nice leaflets, too.

PLEB 2 Yes. Simple, straightforward text and colourful layout.

PLEB 1 Very persuasive. Very.

PLEB 2 Oh, look. Two more platforms.

PLEB 1 We must wait here and listen to what they have to say.

PLEB 2 And get more leaflets.

PLEB 1 You've got ten already.

PLEB 2 I like them.

Enter PFP 1 and 2, who leap onto one of the platforms.

PFP 1 Vote for us!

PFP 2 The Party For Parties!

PLEB 1	Sounds very frivolous.
PLEB 2	What are your policies?
PFP 1	Well, peace for the world, obviously. And having a good time.
PFP 2	Via the establishing of parties every week.
PLEB 2	What would be the benefit of that?
PFP 1	Parties bring people together.
PFP 2	And make them bond better with a bit of song and dance.
PLEB 1	Song and dance? Oo, I don't like the sound of that.
PLEB 2	I think it sounds quite nice.
PLEB 1	How can serious situations be negotiated with a person covered in streamers singing 'Greased Lightning'?
PLEB 2	But there wouldn't be any serious situations to negotiate as people would be a lot happier constantly mingling in the weekly party situations. *(To PFP 1 and 2)* Isn't that right?
PFP 1	That's right.
PFP 2	Here. Do take one of our campaign leaflets. *(Hands Pleb 2 a leaflet.)*
PLEB 2	A leaflet! Excellent! *(Reads.)* Hmm . . . Free pop, cake, jelly and ice-cream every Friday. Free badges, balloons and bunting. Party CDs, sequined clothes and funny hats.
PLEB 1	Sounds silly. Government should be more aggressive. Power is force!

BEU 1 and 2 enter and leap onto the second platform.

BEU 1	Vote for us! We of the BEU Party –
BEU 2	The Beat 'Em Up Party! Beat 'em up and lay 'em out!

BEU 1	Yes! Power is force! Force is power!
PLEB 2	And your policies are . . . ?
BEU 1	Don't take no for an answer!
BEU 2	Fight for your rights!
BEU 1	Flatten with batons!
BEU 2	Walking round the streets in cop-gangs!
BEU 1	Keeping order with threats and menaces!
BEU 2	And big sticks!
BEU 1	Whilst kitted out in exceptionally fashionable leather jackets! Image being very important in politics.
PLEB 1	Excellent! And do you think you'll actually hurt people?
BEU 2	No. They'll just submit because we look so hard.
PLEB 2	Well, I think it all sounds too nasty and violent and I shan't be voting for you.
BEU 1	That's up to you. It's your democratic right to choose.
PLEB 1	*(to Pleb 2)* Yes. Be a wimp and vote for a bunch of party nitwits.
PLEB 2	And you be a zombie and vote for that bunch of biker animals.
PLEB 1	I will!
PLEB 2	And so will I!
PLEB 1	It's a free country!
PLEB 2	It's a democracy!
PLEB 1	Freedom of choice!
PLEB 2	Freedom of expression!
DT	*(entering) Stop!*
EVERYONE ELSE	Stop? Who *is* this person?

DT	My name is Dick Tator!
PFP 1	Dick Tator?
PFP 2	You're joking!
BEU 1	No-one's called that.
BEU 2	Is that as in Po Tator?
PLEB	From which can be made really oppressive chips?
DT	No. As in I am taking over.
EVERYONE ELSE	What?
PFP 1	But you can't. We're having a democratic bit of canvassing here.
DT	But I can. This election is *over!*
PFP 2	But why? You can't do that!
DT	I can because I have *this!* (**Shows them a peculiar device with big springs, wires and lights coming off it.**)
	Everyone jumps and huddles together at the sight of it.
PLEB 1	Agh! He's got a Dimensional Expansion Device!
PLEB 2	The infamous and outlawed form of torture which increases your body-size to that of an elephant!
DT	Forcing your clothes to reach a critical level of Taut Tension 300 Critical Level at which they explode! Yes! *That* device!
PFP 1 AND 2	Our sequins!
BEU 1 AND 2	Our leather!
PFP 1	These outfits were very expensive!
BEU 1	You can't just explode them!
DT	That's just what the *red* button does if I press it. The *green* button neutralises your brain. Which in your case wouldn't take long!

BEU 2 You can't do that! You can't threaten people with an outlawed torture device. It's illegal. The people have a right to be protected!

PFP 2 What about democracy? The people have already chosen to be protected from the evils of that machine. *That's* why it was voted to be outlawed, you silly Tator!

PLEB 1 And what about our freedom of choice? We have the right to vote for whoever we want.

PLEB 2 Including party politics and voting for a good thrashing with a big stick! It's our democratic right!

DT Rubbish. Real power is control via wicked and unfair means. Real threats. Real consequences. Real pain.

PLEB 1 But that's not fair.

DT I don't want to be fair. I want my own way.

PLEB 2 Everyone has the right to *vote* in their own way!

DT When people are given free choice, look what they do with it. Sequins and people with a stick-fetish. It's like being governed by the cast of a West End musical! Someone superior has to take control. Someone with a vision!

PLEB 1 And what's your vision?

DT To have total power and take over the world.

PLEB 2 And how will that benefit mankind?

DT It won't. It'll benefit me.

PLEB 1 What are your policies?

DT I haven't got any.

PLEB 1 So all you've got is that machine and a lot of terror?

DT That's right.

EVERYONE ELSE Oh.

They all look at each other – then drag Dick Tator
offstage. There is the sound of lots of thuds and crashes.

PLEB 1 (*offstage*) Get him!

PLEB 2 (*offstage*) Pin him to the ground!

PFP 1 (*offstage*) Get the machine!

PFP 2 (*offstage*) Ow! That's my arm!

BEU 1 (*offstage*) Sorry.

They all run back on stage, Dick Tator tied up with a
bucket on his head.

BEU 2 (*holding machine*) Got it!

DT How dare you oppress me! You've got no right!

BEU 2 (*removing bucket*) Do you want me to press the green button?

DT No.

BEU 2 Then be quiet.

DT Okay. But this is totally unfair. I've got democratic rights, I have. (*Bucket replaced.*)

PLEB 1 Well, we win, but is this democracy?

PLEB 2 Shouldn't he be allowed to think as he chooses?

PFP 1 Not if it means he stops others from thinking as *they* choose, no.

PFP 2 He is very uncool and not a party person at all.

BEU 1 And he has no dress sense.

PLEB 1 He's mad, he is.

PLEB 2 He hasn't even got a leaflet to hand out!

BEU 2 Dictators! Who'd vote for them?

Healing

List of Characters

Roz

Cara

Ryan

Roz, Cara and Ryan each standing in their own spotlight.
A fourth spotlight is lit, containing a rose, a man's jacket and
a book.

ROZ He died last week. Only last week. Fast asleep in his own chair. I didn't even know he'd gone.

CARA I was distraught when I got the call. I just kept thinking, this isn't true, this isn't happening. It was only a week ago. It feels like a lifetime of agony in seven days.

RYAN My grandad died last week. We all went on a plane ride. I sat by the window so that I could see everything. It was so exciting up there in the clouds!

ROZ The terrible everyday organisation of the funeral. No time to break my heart. Just things to do and relatives to look after . . .

CARA I got over there as soon as I could with Ryan. Simon stayed at home with Laura. She had exams. She couldn't come. I knew that if I took Ryan with me, Simon wouldn't have to worry about picking him up from school and all that other stuff. It was actually a blessing to have him there. He was so oblivious to it all and needed looking after. It kept me from going under. Kept me busy. I didn't have time to cry. Mum was so upset she'd switched onto auto-pilot to cope with it, mechanically doing all that she had to do. I saw her crying one day. The tears were silently pouring from her . . .

and she didn't even know. She just carried on sweeping up the kitchen.

RYAN   I got to meet lots of relatives I'd never met before. They were very nice. They did this funny thing of sometimes they were crying . . . and then sometimes they were all having a laugh and a joke together. I didn't know that people could laugh at funerals. Nanny didn't laugh though. I gave her a flower and a kiss to make her feel better.

Roz puts a flower into one of the buttonholes of her cardigan and smiles at Ryan.

ROZ   I pray that these feelings will leave me. The terrible ache of wanting him back. The terrible knowing that he won't be back. I feel empty, then I feel the oppressive weight of grief suffocating me, then I feel rage at him having left me . . . Then sometimes I feel . . . absolutely nothing.

CARA   I watched Mum really going through the mill. We talked and cried a lot together. We sorted through his things together – though she wanted to sort through his clothes on her own. I understood. The rest of the family were very supportive. Shopping. Get-togethers. They were wonderful.

RYAN   I helped to clean Nanny's car with Uncle Rod and his son Terry. Me and Terry played together a lot. He's got lots of games I haven't got. He's promised to write to me and we are going to e-mail each other as well when we're allowed to.

Time passes. They all change spotlights.

ROZ   Six months later and time is not healing anything. Prayer is – and getting on with all the things I have to do. I'm worried for Cara, however. I don't think she is coping too well at the moment.

CARA I don't think Mum is coping too well at the moment. I'm worried for her. Living in a different country is difficult. I want to be with her, but my family need me here. We talk every day on the phone and once a month I go over – which is a terrible drain on our resources, but Simon insists.

RYAN Mum and Dad are rowing at the moment. I heard Mum say that she couldn't forgive herself over Grandad. Dad said she was being stupid and that kicking herself in the . . . Well, in the bottom . . . wasn't going to bring him back.

ROZ Cara and Max weren't on good terms before he died. They never had a chance to make up. It was a silly row.

CARA It was a stupid row. I'd told him about the extension I was having on the house and he'd moaned about getting myself into debt. And I'd had to have the last word, hadn't I? When he said didn't I care about Ryan, I'd had to say hadn't he cared about us? Living in a poky squat for years so that he could run that charity hostel. He said . . . I said . . . It was a stupid row.

RYAN Mum and Grandad used to argue sometimes, but it never bothered me. But I don't like it when Mum and Dad argue. That's different.

ROZ If it wasn't one thing with those two, it was another.

CARA I should never have said it.

RYAN She said a really bad thing to him the other night.

ROZ I have this photo of them together. She's seven years old and hugging him on the beach.

CARA I told him he was a rotten father.

RYAN She told Dad that she didn't know why she'd married him.

ROZ It's a lovely photo. And the one of them together in his precious rose garden. He named one after her because she loved it so much.

CARA   I want to rip the memory from my mind.

RYAN   I ran upstairs and cried.

ROZ   They loved each other very much. They just clashed. He liked his own way and she was exactly the same.

CARA   I just want to tell him I'm sorry. That I didn't mean it.

RYAN   Don't they know that when they say things like that they hurt me?

Time passes. They change spotlights.

ROZ   A year. Has it really been that long? I was able to look at his photo for the first time yesterday without sobbing. I've lost a lot of weight, but I'm managing to get my bearings again. Managing to ease back into the world. Getting fully involved with the centre again. I realised I'd become a ghost. No husband. No socialising. No point. I was haunting my own house. Then I felt Max's presence in the room. Telling me to get off my –

RYAN   Bottom.

ROZ   And do something. I started to feel more peaceful after that. I couldn't carry on like I was. Max didn't want me to mourn for him forever. The centre put me back on track. I helped this man who'd walked into the centre with his young son. Suddenly bereaved, redundant and homeless. But strong. Determined to carry on. I found him a place. He was so grateful. It helped heal my sadness just to see him and his son move in there. I also booked a ticket to go and see Cara.

CARA   Simon's staying on later at work, I know he is, and I'm relieved by it, to be honest. When we're together, all we do is row. He just can't seem to say anything that doesn't annoy me. I am angry – and then angry about being angry. And I take it all out on Simon. He says what shall we have for tea tonight, and I say dirt for all I care. He says let's go to some party or other, and I say why doesn't he go with someone who'd appreciate a good time because it isn't me. I threw a book at him the other day. He was telling me I'd got to sort myself out and I yelled at him that he was selfish like my father. Except that the book hit Ryan. I felt so awful about it. I shouted at Simon. Told him it was his fault, then went up to see Ryan . . . but he wouldn't let me in. I feel so awful . . .

RYAN   I asked if I could go and stay with my auntie.

CARA   I was so hurt.

RYAN   I said that she'd always said that I could stay with her any time I wanted to.

CARA   I couldn't say no. I looked at that bruise on his forehead and I slowed right down. All the anger turned into remorse. Regret. Wanting him to forgive me. He wouldn't let me help him to pack a few things. I watched him walk out to Viv's car. I stared after the car until the last moment as it disappeared round the corner. He didn't even wave.

RYAN   I know it was an accident, but I just wanted to be away from it for a while and play with my cousins. Auntie's got a big garden and they've got lots of things to do there. When we got there, we all had hot chocolate and biscuits, then played on the climbing frame.

CARA   I cried.

ROZ   When I got to Cara's, Ryan wasn't there and Cara was sobbing. She looked so pale. Cara wouldn't speak for ages, so Simon took me into another room and told me the whole story. I couldn't believe that this had happened in our family. I stormed in to Cara and yelled at her for hurting Ryan. Who did she think she was taking her personal grief out on other people? Grieving is one thing, but refusing to deal with it and lashing out at an innocent instead is another. I told her: when was she going to get a grip and deal with her feelings about Max?

CARA It's too late.

ROZ It is not too late.

CARA How can I say I'm sorry to a dead man?

ROZ Pray.

CARA I don't believe.

ROZ But you believe in torturing your husband and hitting your child?

CARA That was an accident!

ROZ You've got enough time to meditate on all your negative feelings and feel sorry for yourself!

CARA It was an accident!

ROZ I know! And so was what you said to your father. When are you going to realise that?

CARA I didn't mean what I said to him.

ROZ I know.

CARA (*moving into Roz's spotlight*) I did love him. I just wanted to keep him more to myself rather than share him with everyone else. I was just being selfish. I do still love him.

ROZ (*hugging her daughter*) He knows.

Ryan moves into the spotlight that has the book. It is a photograph album. He turns its pages as he speaks.

RYAN I found a photo album of Auntie's. Auntie talked me through it and told me who everyone was. She told me about Grandad, of how he was in the army once and that's why he was wearing a uniform in one picture. She said I looked a lot like him. She showed me a photo of him when he was a little boy. (*Stops at this photo.*) I suppose I do a bit. But I'm me. (*Turns the page and stops again.*) She showed me a photo of the house he set up for poor people who had no home to stay in. He would help them to find jobs and then they would move out when they could look after themselves. I think Grandad was very kind. I asked Auntie why Mummy was always unhappy about him and she said that Mummy sometimes felt that Grandad had more time for the people at the centre than he did for her. But that wasn't true. Grandad was just busy.

Time passes. They swap spotlights again.

RYAN   We've been on a plane again!

ROZ   I told them to come and spend their summer holiday with me. Not only could Cara spend some time with Simon while I looked after Ryan and Laura, she could also help out at the centre and see how other people grieved, worried and still got on with their lives. She could start making peace with her father's memory, too, being back in the old family home where they'd spent so much time together that she'd forgotten about. She has to heal by getting a clear picture of her relationship with her father, but also see all the good things he did for the community. She needs to realise that he wasn't rejecting her. She needs . . . to remember the love.

Cara moves into the spotlight that has the photograph album and starts turning its pages, then touches the rose.

Good

List of Characters

Ian

Ewan

Holly

Diz

Donna

Classroom. After-school meeting of the committee organising a disco to raise funds for a charity. All present except for Donna.

IAN Donna's late. As usual. Having a fag at the back of K-Block with Jaz, I suppose.

EWAN She'll be here.

HOLLY Stop sticking up for her, Ewan, just 'cause you fancy her.

DIZ Donna is not the issue of this committee meeting. The charity disco for the hospice is. Let's stay on track. So – going back to what we were talking about – we need a new DJ.

HOLLY This is looking a mess already. Another DJ and having to do it on the Saturday? We don't know any other DJs as cheap as him and –

DONNA (*entering*) Sorry I'm late. I had to hand in some coursework. (*To someone outside.*) About half-an-hour by the shops. Okay?

HOLLY Good of you to come, Donna. And yeah, you are late. Got anything to say?

DONNA I couldn't help it. (*Goes to sit by Ewan, who puts his bag on the chair so that she can' t. She sits by Diz, who pulls a face of mock thanks to Ewan.*)

HOLLY   (*delighted that Donna just got frozen out by Ewan*) Well, nice
        to see you anyway. You're here just in time to hear about
        the collapse of the charity disco.

EWAN   It isn't going to collapse.

HOLLY   Do you know of another DJ that's as cheap as Doyle's mate?

EWAN   Does anyone know anyone as dodgy as Doyle's mate?

DONNA   You're being a bit aggressive, aren't you, Ewan? What's up
        with you?

EWAN   Nothing's up with me.

DIZ   (*keeping on task*) We'll ask around.

DONNA   What's the matter with the usual DJ?

HOLLY   You see? It's just a waste of time, the whole thing! It's
        falling apart before it's begun and Donna can't even get
        herself here on time. There's no commitment!

IAN   Shut up, Holly. That's not helping.

DONNA   (*insistent that she is answered*) *What's* the matter with the
        usual DJ?

HOLLY   The police are investigating him for drugs!

DONNA   Well I only *asked*, Holly!

IAN   You've got no right to start on Holly, Donna.

DONNA   I'm not starting on Holly, *Ian*.

IAN   You couldn't even get here on time, what with messing
        about behind K-Block.

DONNA   Who says I was?

IAN   Meet you at the shops! We all heard you talking to Jaz.

DONNA   I wasn't!

IAN   It's a bit stupid to do it in front of everyone if you don't
        want everyone to know!

EWAN   Shut up the both of you! Is this a youth club committee
        or a blazing session? Have you forgotten what we're here

for? This is serious to me even if it isn't to you. We're doing this for the hospice up the road, not for you to get a stage for your stinking egos!

Silence.

DIZ   (*calmly*) Let's get back to the fund-raising. Right, let's jot down what there isn't a problem with. Tickets?

HOLLY   Jamie said he'd do them on his computer, no problem, if you just give him the details.

DIZ   Tuck-shop food and drink available as usual?

DONNA   Yeah. I'll organise it with the duty staff that night. And we'll put a donation tin next to the tuck in case anyone's got any spare cash on them.

DIZ   Is that pushing it too much?

DONNA   You've just got to turn on the old seductive girly-charm, Diz.

HOLLY   Well, you'd know all about that –

IAN   Shut up, Holly.

DIZ   And you've got to find out which staff are up for duty that night and thank them in advance because this is an extra youth club we're putting on.

DONNA   They get paid.

IAN   Donna! You are such a –

DIZ   (*keeping it calm*) They don't have to do it. And they don't get that much. I wouldn't do it for the money.

DONNA   You're so good.

DIZ   (*ignoring that*) And if we've got to do it on Saturday –

HOLLY   No!

DIZ   If we've got to do it on Saturday, can we?

HOLLY   But –

DIZ   *Can* we?

IAN   Yes, we can.

DONNA   I can.

IAN   There. Donna can. Grab the opportunity. She's made you an offer you can't refuse.

EWAN   I'll be the contact with the hospice with Diz. We'll also report back to the Head with any new details when we deliver the minutes to her. So it's just the DJ and the day itself.

HOLLY   Why didn't you push harder with the Head on the day? You were in the School Council meeting with her. You knew you could do it. What happened?

IAN   What is this with Saturday, exactly?

HOLLY   No-one's ever around on Saturday. Everyone round here mostly goes over to the Action Network – the new leisure complex on the outskirts of town. No-one's going to come to youth club on the biggest night of the week. I told you that before you went in.

EWAN   The Head insisted that there would be no-one to staff it on the Thursday night, because Wednesday night is Parents' Evening and they'd want a night off afterwards.

HOLLY   Great.

DONNA   Teachers have got lives too, you know, Holly.

HOLLY   I don't really need to be told this by you, actually, Donna. And how come you can do a Saturday night anyway? You can barely turn up on time for a weekday meeting.

DONNA   This disco's important.

HOLLY   Why?

DONNA   I know someone in the hospice.

IAN   Who?

DONNA   A neighbour . . . You don't know them.

Silence. Donna and Ewan look at each other.

DIZ Maybe the way round it is just to postpone the disco until later on next half-term.

DONNA We need to go back to the school calendar, then, and start trekking through the dates again.

EWAN Avoiding Parents' Evenings like the plague.

DIZ There's only one next half-term, isn't there? Most of them are on this side of the holiday.

HOLLY It just can't be a Saturday, that's all I'm saying.

IAN Yeah, we heard you the first ten times you said it, Holly.

EWAN And Ian'll have to liaise with Truman about the DJ.

IAN Me liaise with Truman?

EWAN About getting another DJ. It'd be a good idea before you meet with him to ask around the kids for names and look in the phone book. Maybe we can get a subsidy from School Fund for any extra the new one may charge.

IAN Truman hates me! He put me in detention last week.

EWAN What for?

IAN Late coursework.

DONNA I always get mine in on time.

IAN Shut up, Donna.

DIZ And was it late?

IAN Yes, but I had a very busy week last week . . .

EWAN Yeah, and your dog ate it. Just liaise with him, Ian. We've all got to do our bit. Truman's all right.

DIZ Yeah, Truman's good to work with. The Deputy's always in contact with the money and everyone else who's in contact with the money. And he's always easy to approach. Not like Barlow.

IAN Him? He blew my head off last time I asked him for help. I thought he had a shotgun under the desk. Said he was busy.

HOLLY What was he like at the Year Council meeting?

EWAN Putting up with it. He thinks kids shouldn't be involved in the running of the school. Thinks we're not mature enough. Thinks we don't care enough about the school and the community because we're too busy with ourselves. So we have to continue to prove him wrong. Don't we?

Suffering

List of Characters

Nash

Azzy

Rod

Break-time. Seating area. Azzy enters and sits down looking miserable. Nash storms in.

NASH Oy. Loser. Thanks for wasting everyone's time.

AZZY I didn't mean to.

NASH Didn't mean to make us all look stupid, you mean.

AZZY I'm not feeling too good.

NASH I don't care how you feel. Thinking of yourself all the time. Typical. That's all you ever do.

AZZY I didn't ask to be in your group. The teacher did that.

NASH A great pity.

AZZY I'm sorry.

NASH Sorry's not good enough.

AZZY Well, what else do you want me to do?

NASH Suffer. Like the rest of us. Two weeks we spent researching and working on that presentation. And what did you do to help us? Nothing.

AZZY I tried my best.

NASH You just sat there, promising that you'd do stuff at home, but now – obviously – I see that that wasn't the case.

AZZY You don't understand . . .

NASH I understand that you don't take anything seriously. You might think schoolwork is a right laugh, but I don't. Not

---

when we had to present such serious stuff. The trials and troubles of the people in Ghana is a serious issue. And we all took it seriously.

AZZY   (*fighting back*) Apart from me.

NASH   Exactly!

AZZY   I did do the research. I was the one who researched that village in Ghana, the poverty of the people, the suffering due to their cash-and-carry economy . . .

NASH   Oh! It's coming out now, is it?

AZZY   I did the research. The women breaking boulders for 20,000 cedis – two quid – a week, hardly any money for food, everything having to be paid for. Water from a borehole for 250 cedis a go. All visits to the hospital and treatment having to be paid for or they're not allowed to leave. They even have to pay to use the public toilet. I know. I know how those people suffer. I did the research!

NASH   But it wasn't any good to us at your house, was it?

AZZY   I did it. I wrote it all down. All about the privatisation, the way the mining companies are pushing people off their farmland to mine it for gold – I did all of it.

NASH   And it was so important that you left it at home. You should have been memorising your notes like everyone else had to do. Even if you'd left your notes at home, it shouldn't have mattered.

AZZY   Well, I didn't.

NASH   You never take anything seriously. That's why you got put with us in the first place: to force you to work. Well, now you've wrecked our work and we've lost a grade because of it!

AZZY   The teacher will let you two do it again, you know she will.

NASH   That's not the point!

Enter Rod.

ROD   Enough.

NASH   Two weeks' work down the toilet!

ROD   I said enough. You've had your say, Nash.

NASH   (*to Azzy*) Schoolwork's not a joke. Not to me. When I work
hard at something, I want a result. You made me look
foolish today. The class laughed at us. And all the research
and follow-on from your section that Rod did on Fairtrade
was lost. Because there was nothing to follow on from. So
why Rod's sticking up for you now, I don't know.

ROD   What went wrong, Azzy, you're not usually like this?

NASH   Azzy's been like this for ages now. (*To Azzy*) Not got into
enough trouble with the teachers yet? Want to drag us lot
down with you?

AZZY   What do you want? A fight? 'Cause I can't think of another
reason why you're still here, moaning on and on about the
same thing.

NASH   Fight you? Your immaturity makes me puke. You've got no
sense of responsibility. You don't care that what you do
affects other people. And I'm not wasting any more of my
time talking to you. (*Exits.*)

Silence.

AZZY   I hate Nash.

ROD   For being angry?

AZZY   For being right. (*Preparing for a telling-off.*) Your turn now,
I see, Rod. I'll start, shall I? Sorry for wrecking your big
speech about Fairtrade and the community-friendly coffee
business with the Chiapas people in Mexico.

ROD   What's the matter?

AZZY   I'll bet it was going to be good. I'll bet you memorised all
your notes and had a few visual aids to display.

ROD   Yeah. What's wrong?

AZZY	What grade do you think you'd have got? A? A*?
ROD	G. Are you going to talk to me or what?

Silence.

AZZY	(*sad and frustrated*) I did the research. I just couldn't focus enough to learn it.
ROD	What happened to your hand?
AZZY	I hurt it.
ROD	How?
AZZY	I've started digging into it recently. I get numb. This checks that I can still feel something.
ROD	Why?
AZZY	My parents are divorcing.
ROD	I didn't know. I'm sorry.
AZZY	I'll deal with it. At least they won't be fighting any more. The rows were terrible. He hated her. She hated him. They wished they'd never met. He knew what happened that weekend and she certainly knew about the party. And whose idea was it to have kids anyway? (*Pause, then hurt.*) Didn't they know I was listening?
ROD	How are you coping?
AZZY	(*laughs, ironically*) Really well, don't you think?
ROD	Are you all right at home?
AZZY	Dad left a few weeks ago. I'm not eating that much, but I can sleep for England! And play up. Rows with Mum about anything – because I think she needs to cry a bit more, you know. I've been really helpful to her like that. Plus loads of really cool stuff at school like back-answering teachers, messing about in class, not doing my work . . . (*hurting*) Because I'm doing anything to block out the reality of what's happening.

ROD You should have told someone. I'd have listened.

AZZY Then it'd all be real, wouldn't it? No-one knew at school, so everything was normal here.

ROD Apart from you going AWOL from your brain.

AZZY You're not supposed to tease depressed people.

ROD You're not depressed. You're divorced.

AZZY Me?

ROD Well, your dad's left you, too, hasn't he?

AZZY Still, what am I moaning about? Loads of kids in this school have been through the same thing. Look at Foster. His dad walked out, then her next partner did, then her next. I mean, just as Foster had got attached to them, formed some bond of trust with them, they were off again. But he seems all right with it. He's got used to it.

ROD Yeah. That's why he's chain-smoking and won't talk to anyone. He's got a cough like an old man. It's like he's trying to surround himself with smoke so that people can't get through to him.

AZZY I know how he feels. I'm on my own. I want to tell Mum, but she's got work, shopping, the baby . . . I help out. Try to get through to her that way. But she's all isolated inside, too. She feels like me. Unloved. Somehow, at some point, the love got disconnected and the supply wasn't reaching any of us in the end. Except for Dad. He got reconnected somewhere else.

ROD Has your mum got someone to talk to?

AZZY Yeah. She's always on the phone to her mates, or I baby-sit while she goes to see them. But I just can't open up to people like she can.

ROD You're doing all right now.

AZZY (*suddenly realising*) Oh. Yeah. You're right. Why are you listening to all this? I just screwed up your big speech.

ROD   We're friends. You talk. I listen. You're sorted. I'm happy. Like Fairtrade really.

AZZY   (*smiling*) Trust you to bring it back to the lesson! (*Pause.*) Do you think Dad'll come back?

ROD   Even if he did, it'd be different. The old pieces aren't going to fit back together again. When my mum came back, everything had to change because everything was different.

AZZY   It helps to talk to you – even though I don't get what the hell you're on about half the time.

Bell rings.

ROD   I'll meet you at dinnertime.

AZZY   I won't feel like eating.

ROD   Good. You pay for it and I'll eat it.

AZZY   What?

ROD   You see? You've just got to see things differently.

AZZY   I suppose I should think of what I've got rather than what I haven't. Those people in Ghana suffer terribly . . . and their kids. Maybe I could look into raising money for them. Do you want to help? It'd take my mind off my own worries some.

ROD   Okay. And talk to your mum. Open up to her. How's she going to know how you feel if you don't tell her?

They head off for next lesson.

AZZY   I still love my dad, you know.

ROD   Good. Love's always good. It shows you care.

Business

List of Characters

Slater

Grage

Travis

Wilson

Deel

A new building has been erected in a small town.

SLATER   The perfect place. An old industrial town that lost its industry a long time ago.

GRAGE   What was the industry here?

SLATER   Steel.

GRAGE   Oh. Pre-historic industry.

SLATER   It was what this area was good at. Your generation doesn't remember.

GRAGE   What was the problem?

SLATER   Complacency. If only the owners had invested in the latest technology and modernised, there'd be a massive foundry complex here now. The biggest in Amivia. Maybe.

GRAGE   Why maybe?

SLATER   *(reflectively)* Well, the government never did have much time for steel.

GRAGE   The Federated States make all the steel now, don't they?

SLATER   Most of it. They modernised you see. Then, when Amivia joined the FS, the steel-making got shared out. And Amivia –

GRAGE   – not having the modernised machinery –

SLATER – didn't get the work.

GRAGE Management error, workforce punished, eh?

SLATER And we got this piece of land cheap.

GRAGE So, there's an up-side to everything, Slater.

SLATER There is, Grage, my boy, there is. Goodbye, local industry and hello, consumer warehousing.

GRAGE It's a fine warehouse, isn't it? Our prices are so cheap, we'll make quite a killing. And the warehouse club-membership card will ensure that they regularly buy from us instead of the other supermarkets and hypermarkets in the area. We've sold thirty thousand already.

SLATER And at twenty FS credits a card, that's – six hundred thousand.

GRAGE We're rich already without even opening the doors!

SLATER Not rich enough. Not yet.

GRAGE What do you mean, not yet?

SLATER I received a few calls this morning. The representatives of the chief executive officers of the surrounding supermarkets and hypermarkets, no less, are meeting us here.

GRAGE When?

SLATER Round about . . . (*Looks at watch.*) Now. And here they come. Nice cars.

GRAGE You never told me about this, Slater.

SLATER There's a lot of things I don't tell you about, son.

GRAGE Why do you patronise me so much?

SLATER Because I pay your wages, lad. Now smile. We're on.

Enter Travis, Wilson and Deel.

SLATER You're very prompt.

TRAVIS	We're very business-like.
WILSON	But then, that's why were here.
DEEL	Business. Well, what business is it that you have in mind, Mr Slater?
SLATER	I believe, from your communications with me over the past month, that my new warehouse is causing you a few problems.
TRAVIS	I wouldn't use the word 'problems', Mr Slater.
WILSON	We would just like you to reconsider setting up in this area.
DEEL	With regard to the wider business community.
SLATER	The wider business community? You, you mean. And in what way would you like me to reconsider?
TRAVIS	Our businesses are the main suppliers of food and general commodities to the local area.
WILSON	And we don't appreciate competing with you.
DEEL	As I'm sure you will understand, Mr Slater. Being a business person yourself.
SLATER	Oh, I do. I certainly do, Ms . . . ?
DEEL	Deel. Senior representative of Deelmarkets supermarket chain. Myself, Mr Travis and Mr Wilson are keen to resolve this situation as soon as possible.
SLATER	The situation being that my warehouse is going to take business away from you.
TRAVIS	Quite.
WILSON	We are confident that you will be co-operative, Mr Slater.
SLATER	(*to Grage*) When do our doors open, Colin?
GRAGE	The 21st of this month, Mr Slater. Very soon now.
SLATER	Very soon indeed. (*To Travis*) So, what do you suggest?

TRAVIS	Fifty million credits to close down and clear out of the area.
SLATER	Fifty million? Please. Do not waste my time. I'm a busy man. What do you say, Colin?
GRAGE	An insult to your status within the business community, Mr Slater.
DEEL	Status? What status? You're a fly-by-night merchant, Slater. Don't think yourself to be even in the same league as my colleagues and I!
SLATER	I don't think I'm really in a mood to take this meeting this morning, Colin. What else is on our agenda? Good morning to you.
WILSON	(*swiftly*) Eighty million. We give you a month to open and sell off your stock, then you give out to the press about cash-flow problems.
DEEL	And you close on the 21st of the following month.
SLATER	An interesting proposal. (*Pause, then smugly.*) I'll think about it.
DEEL	What? (*Moves to lay hands on Slater.*)
TRAVIS	(*stopping Deel*) When will we be hearing from you, Mr Slater? Tomorrow morning would be convenient. At around 9.30? Without fail?
SLATER	You have my word. (*Smiles broadly.*) As a gentleman.
TRAVIS	Good morning, Mr Slater.
	Travis, Wilson and Deel exit.
GRAGE	You never intended to open at all, did you? Isn't this all rather dishonest and corrupt?
SLATER	Business, Grage, my boy, is business.

Fantasy

List of Characters

Kid I

Kid 2

Kid 3

Careers Officer

Three teenagers in one spotlight, talking round a table. A careers officer is in a separate spotlight, addressing the audience.

K1
K2 I hate school.
K3

K1 All the projects and practicals. And homework! Can't wait till I leave.

K2 What you gonna do?

K3 Anything's gotta be better than this.

K1 I'm gonna be an engineer.

K2 Are you?

K3 Engineer. That's a good job, that is. Lots of money.

K1 I know.

CO Engineer. An excellent career for well-organised, logical people who like solving problems and planning solutions.

K2 Sounds good. Do you need Maths?

K1 No. My uncle knows an engineer. He'll get me in.

CO The job requires good IT and numeracy skills, plus the ability to work positively with others.

K1 Are you listening to me, you dork?

κ3   I'm taking my pen apart!

κ1   Just listen, will ya? You get a big company car and a load of people working for you on a building site.

κ2   You mean, you just tell them what to do and they do it? Cool.

κ3   What's an engineer do anyway?

co   A planning engineer – one of many different kinds of engineer – is the co-ordinator of a large construction project. He or she is the person who makes sure that the job is carried out correctly and that all resources are used cost-efficiently. They also work closely with managers and staff to ensure that the project is problem-free and on schedule.

κ1   It's easy. There's not that much to it.

κ2   Is it a long day?

K1   No. Nine till five. I might just do it part-time though.

κ3   So plenty of time to go out after in your big car.

κ1   Yeah.

κ2   You can pick us up then.

κ1   I'll think about it. I might be going for a ride in my jet.

co   A planning engineer, in theory, has a forty-hour week, but basically they have to continue until the work is finished. It is not a part-time occupation.

κ3   Do you need any exams?

κ1   No. I'll just do a course at college.

co   The entry requirement is a degree or BTEC/SQA HND course, for which you will need five GCSE A to C passes with two A-Levels.

κ1   So there's no point doing all this schoolwork.

co   Alternatively, you could at sixteen gain student registration with the Chartered Institute of Building and work towards the Institute's exams whilst employed. The entry requirement to do this is four GCSE A to C grades and one A-level before taking the CIOB exam.

K2 Will the course take long to do?

K1 I'm not staying on at college for any more than a year.

CO It is possible to achieve the CIOB exam in about six years.

K2 I'm gonna be an architect.

K1 I was thinking of that, but an engineer's easier. Like the one in that advert who uses the right shampoo and has a really flash apartment. He's got his own bar, a jacuzzi and loads of women.

K2 Women?

K1 Oh, yeah. Women fancy engineers all right. Can't keep their hands off them.

K2 What about women engineers?

K1 Well, they like men engineers, don't they? Of course. Stupid.

K3 What's an architect?

K2 Don't you know anything? It's somebody who draws buildings.

CO An architect designs, redesigns or alters buildings, both old and new. This also involves the spacing and layout of the buildings on site.

K2 I like drawing.

K1 Like what?

K2 Cartoon stuff mostly. I'm really good at them.

K3 Yeah. They're all over your exercise book, aren't they? Well, they were. The teacher made you stay in and cover your book and everyone else's as a punishment, didn't he?

K2 I don't remember that.

CO An interest in creativity, the arts and the skill of thinking in three dimensions. Organisational, planning and budgeting skills are also an advantage.

K2   I colour them in as well. With Tipp-ex.

K1   Ah, well, you're an artist, aren't you? No felts?

K2   No. I had some spare cash, but I bought some crisps instead. What we got this afternoon?

K3   Science.

K2   I hate Science. I'll be glad when I don't have to do it any more. I mean, what's the point of it? I'm glad I don't need it to be an architect.

CO   Architects need to understand how buildings are affected by heat, light, ventilation and sound, in addition to knowledge of all the gas, water and electricity needs plus any resources used.

K2   And IT is worse.

CO   Architects are increasingly moving from the drawing-board to CAD – computer-aided design.

K1   There has to be a lot of study connected to the job. That's why I'm going to be an engineer instead.

K2   I won't need any exams. My uncle's friend's cousin is an architect. He'll get me in.

CO   The minimum entry requirements for this career are five GCSE A to C passes or S grades 1 to 3, which must include English, Maths and Science qualifications, followed by three A levels or H grades, including a Maths or Science qualification. Most schools of architecture will require a portfolio of drawings or sketches to support your application.

K2   I reckon in a couple of years I'll be able to afford my own yacht.

CO   Students will be awarded a degree after three years of study in a school of architecture, at which time they will spend a year in an architect's office. Further study and professional experience of approximately three years' duration will lead to a professional practice examination.

K2 It'll be a doddle. (*To K3*) What do you want to be?

K3 I've thought about being a lawyer.

co Solicitor? Private practice? Legal aid? Commercial practice? Crown Prosecution Service? That's the Procurator Fiscal Service in Scotland, of course. The law degree route could be taken, or the Common Professional Examination. Or those who are already in legal employment might apply if they are Members or Fellows of the Institute of Legal Executives.

K3 Or a doctor.

K1 You hate Science.

K3 Or a pop star.

K2 You hate Music.

K3 Or a footballer.

K1 You never bring your kit.

K2 And you're crap at football anyway.

K3 I'm not! . . . That bad.

K2 You live in a fantasy world, you do.

K1 Yeah. Let's face it. You've got to be realistic.

Strengths

List of Characters

Two characters with no names

NOTES:

Is strength purely a matter of physical strength? Can a person be strong in other ways? Who, in the sketch, discovers this?

A   You are so puny.

B   I'm strong enough.

A   Strong enough for what?

B   For whatever it is that I have to do every day.

A   But you're so small.

B   Only compared to you. To an ant, I'm a giant.

A   I've got fine, muscular hind legs. I can't even see your legs.

B   They get me along. All four of them. Same size.
Equally balanced.

A   Are you saying I'm unbalanced?

B   You are so touchy.

A   I can race anything, I can. And beat it.

B   I don't see that as a sign of strength either.

A   Not just strength. Look at these ears. Fantastic radar. I don't even know if you *have* ears.

B   I can hear *you*. Unfortunately.

A   Territorial champ, too. I can fight anybody who comes onto my turf.

B   This is all *physical*. Tut!

A   You couldn't fight anything.

B   I don't *want* to fight anything. I am quite happy the way I am and *that* is where my strength lies. Unlike you. Always trying to prove something.

A   I will not be criticised by something that takes ten hours to eat a piece of lettuce!

B   'Something'? Oo. Getting defensive now as well as aggressive.

A   Hiding in your shell all the time. You're just a scaredy-cat.

B   I'm neither scared nor a cat. My shell is to protect my vulnerable body.

A   It's weak then. Not strong. Admit it! You're weak!

B   No. I have evolved very *sensibly*. I have a vulnerable body, so a very strong shell to protect it. That's why one of my relatives is nearly two hundred years old. Our strength is in our logical and calm evolution.

A   So you're saying *I'm* the weak one? Me? I'm weak? Come on. I'll race you! I'll show you!

B   Oh, very well. But what's it going to prove?

Changes

List of Characters

Three characters with no names

NOTES:
Who is having a conversation in this sketch? What changes do people like to make about themselves? What changes don't they need to make about themselves?

A   I did it! Look! I've changed!

B   Amazing. How did you do that?

A   Trial and error and lots of effort.

B   The spots are disappearing.

A   And I'm getting stripes! Wait till everyone sees! You can change, too, you know.

B   Oh, I'm fine. The tail's a bit small, but the legs get me around and this trunk's great. I'm not bothered about the grey.

C   Oy! You!

B   Hello. Here comes trouble.

C   What do you think you're doing?

B   Just standing here admiring the view.

C   Not you, Water-Snorter.

B   Jealous. Just because *you* can't.

C   I can run better than you.

B   I can stomp on things better than you.

C   Is that a threat?

B   Oh, push off.

C   Anyway, I'm talking to *you*, Changeling.

A   Do you like my new stripes?

C   *We've* got the stripes, not *you*.

B   It's a free country.

C   No, it isn't. And you are well out of order, flaunting those stripes when you are supposed to have spots.

A   I don't see the problem. I fancied a change. The spot-thing was becoming a drag.

C   The spot-thing?

A   I'd wake up every morning – spots. I'd go for a walk and look at myself in a pool – spots. So – predictable.

C   What *are* you on about? The 'spot-thing' is who *you* are. And the 'stripe-thing' is who *I* am. And the 'grey-thing' is who *he* is.

B   It sounds so bland when you say it like that.

A   (*to B*) You could always highlight the grey with something else.

B   Really? Like what?

C   No! No highlighting! We are who we are.

A   Well, who I am wants to change!

C   But you can't change your *skin*! You have spots for a *reason*! I have stripes for a reason. He is grey for a reason – whatever that is.

B   Well, I think it's a sun-thing, actually.

C   Your spots are camouflage – but also elegant and beautiful. They make you who you are. Evolved and natural. Individual.

A   I want stripes!

C   *We've* got the stripes. You're taking from *our* identity – and – losing yours. It's weird. Like growing a trunk.

B   Excuse me!

C   No offence. Just – be *yourself*.

Section 2:
Relationships and Respect
Scripts for the Heart

Empathy
List of Characters

Jon

Marie

Jon and Marie sitting at their desks in separate spotlights, e-mailing each other.

JON Dear Marie. Hi!

MARIE Dear Jon. How are you?

JON It was really nice to hear from you.

MARIE How is your family?

JON My little sister's playing up, as usual!

MARIE My little brother's driving me stupid!

JON I do hope your sister got over the 'flu. There's been a bit of it here, too, but luckily I didn't catch it.

MARIE My sister was really ill with it. We had to get the doctor in. It took him ages – and then we had to queue for the medicine. We don't have to pay for it though. Thank goodness! We couldn't afford it.

JON Have you had your roof fixed yet? Why was it you couldn't get any help?

MARIE The roof got fixed, but only because my uncle did it. He is a good man. We couldn't get anyone else to help. It's just like being ill. Unless you can pay, you've got to wait your turn – and the wait is huge. We couldn't afford the repairs, so in the end my uncle did the best he could with the bits and pieces of wood he'd got. Still, it hasn't leaked yet. Which is amazing when you consider all the terrible rain and storms we've had!

JON   I do hope you were better prepared for the rains this year. We prayed for you, as you know, last year when we saw it on television. We've had our share of bad storms, too. I know what it's like.

MARIE   The floods were terrible last year. Many round here lost most of their possessions and their homes were ruined. Beyond anything they could afford to have repaired. And, of course, there's a wait for compensation. Let's hope it doesn't happen again, but my family are worried. And people are saying that with global warming it may get worse. Oh, dear. Getting too doomy and gloomy! I shall change the subject. Thank you for the lovely hat, by the way! I'm wearing it right now and I look fabulous in it.

JON   I loved the hat you were wearing in the last photo you sent me, and I thought, cool hat! I'll send her another one even more cool! I'm glad you like it. I bought it from the market at the other end of the city. I wanted to go with my friends on our own, but my aunt and uncle insisted on coming with us! They said that that end of the city wasn't safe, bad types, thieves, it's not as safe as where we live – the usual! Relatives!

MARIE   It was so kind of you to think of me. And the hamper was fantastic! We all loved it! Haven't eaten anything so nice in a long time!

JON   We're glad the hamper cheered you up. My grandfather has been cooking and bottling and pickling stuff in the cellar again. We can't stop him and we certainly can't eat it all! You're doing us a favour by having some of it! Look out, as there will undoubtedly be more on its way soon, unless we can restrain Grandad! It'll have to be a strait-jacket! I was so sorry to hear that there was more fighting outside your house again recently, not to mention the burning car. Why do people do it?

MARIE What do they think it solves?

JON Thank goodness you weren't hurt.

MARIE Mum was saying how you had had a lot of trouble in your country at one time, years ago, so many having to leave their homes, but that it's all calmed down now over there. I know there is still some trouble – isn't there everywhere? – but because your hotel is in the suburbs in the better-off part of the city, you're away from it. Your family must have suffered terribly in the past though.

JON It's been a lot better here in recent years. The government's really been sorting things out. The amenities and facilities are so much better now and there's lots of new building going on. Businesses seem to be thriving and everyone's so much into the new technology! Who hasn't got a website?

MARIE I'd really love a computer of my own one day. I use the ones at school, but it's not the same as the freedom of having your own. It's an incredible luxury though at the moment. I have to e-mail you from my friend's house.

JON We contacted the UHPL, who'll set up websites for any one or any business that wants one. They set up a website for the hotel and it's certainly improved business now that we're on-line!

MARIE My uncle lost his job last week. Streamlining, I think they called it. I can't believe so much has happened to us in the past year. There I go again! Change of subject! I'm glad you went on the school trip, by the way, and didn't fake the plague to get out of it as you said you were going to!

JON The city museum! Boring! Cultural heritage work-booklets to fill in. Urgh! Did you get to go on yours?

MARIE Yes, I did get to go on our school trip. There's an excellent support fund been set up within the school for us lot who got whacked by the floods. It's good to know that the community care. The rioters are just a vicious minority.

JON Next month, we're off to the theatre, then there's a big Geography thing – or is it a Biology thing? A tour of the national park. More work-booklets, I'll bet – but elephants and gorillas, too! Wow! Anyway, must go now. Mail me soon.

MARIE Must go now. Mail me soon.

JON Loads of love, Jon.

MARIE Loads of love, Marie.

JON Kampala, Uganda.

MARIE City outskirts, Great Britain.

Help

List of Characters

Samaritan

Victim

The roadside outside of town. A man has been set upon by members of The Kapps, a rival gang to his own, The Montz. He has been left for dead. Another man arrives to help him.

SAM   Here. Let me help you.

VIC   Thanks. I didn't think I was going to make it. The other two just left me here.

SAM   Other two?

VIC   Yeah. They just drove on by and left me here. Ow! Take it easy, will ya? I've nearly been killed once today already.

SAM   Sorry. I'm trying to clean you up. I've got to get you to the nearest town and fast. These wounds are bad.

VIC   I'll say! They must've hit me with a crowbar. Both ends. And did those punks driving past in their fancy cars stop? No.

SAM   Maybe they didn't see you.

VIC   Didn't see me? Are you kidding? Bleeding and yelling for help? They saw me all right. I recognised them, too. Two members of my own gang. Not stopping in case it was an ambush. Left me for dead! My own people!

SAM   Try to keep calm. You're making the blood run faster.

VIC   Keep calm? Hey, give me something to wear, will ya? They ripped my clothes to shreds. I'm cold . . .

SAM   Here's my coat. What happened anyway?

VIC   They were supposed to look after me. I did a job for them. Delivered a gas device to one of The Kapps' main hideouts. You know, smoke 'em out and choke 'em up a bit. A bit of territorial invasion to keep them on their toes.

SAM   (*guessing what happened*) Except that they were waiting for you. Bundled you into a car. Drove you out here. Beat you up.

VIC   I was scared. Especially when they tied the device to me and re-set it to go off when they were gone. Except it never went off. There was a click – the hatch flew up – but no gas came out. It was a set-up. The Montz don't want me in their gang so they sent me out with a dud device to get me beaten up.

SAM   They've probably contacted The Kapps to tell them as well. Just so they don't get a visit. Gang wars. It's all one big game. I've patched you up as best I can. Are you ready to make a move to the car?

VIC   Yeah. I think so. I went through the gang initiation, proved my bravery, had the gang's emblem branded on my arm – Look. Didn't I prove myself enough?

Sam helps Vic up.

VIC   I'm a poor man, but whatever I have is yours. Whatever I can do to pay you back for your help.

SAM   No need.

VIC   You religious or something?

SAM   I'm a Samaritan.

VIC   That lot on the phones you can talk to if you've got problems you want to talk about?

SAM   The very same.

VIC   So you're doing house calls now, are you? (*Smiles at him.*)

SAM   Looks like it, doesn't it? There. You okay so far?

VIC   Yes . . . I . . . The pain, it's getting worse . . .

SAM   Just take it easy . . . Everything'll be fine . . .

VIC   It must be a good feeling to help people. I usually hurt them. Well, I hurt Kapps. But they started it. (*Thinks about this.*) I suppose. Everyone says they did. But then The Kapps say we did. I don't think anyone really knows. Still, that's war.

SAM   No. That's stupid. Right, just ease yourself onto the back seat.

VIC   Thanks. I'm there. Hey! What's that on your arm?

SAM   Nothing. An old mistake.

VIC   It's a gang-emblem brand. You're never . . . (*Looks at brand.*) You're a Kapp!

SAM   (*knowing what will happen now*) *Was* a Kapp.

VIC   (*getting out of the car with effort, horrified*) Get me out of here, man.

SAM   Get back in the car.

VIC   Get into a Kapp's car? Are you crazy? We're sworn enemies! Montz and Kapps. You might have heard. Get away from me. I don't want *your* help.

SAM   But you're bleeding.

VIC   At least it's pure blood. Not part Gentivok, that drug you all take to make you fight more like animals.

SAM   That's not true.

VIC   Denying it means nothing to me. You're a Kapp. That's all I need to know.

SAM   Ex-Kapp. I was – until I grew up.

VIC   You cut each other and do devil-stuff or something . . . and I'd rather die than be helped by you!

SAM   I haven't been a Kapp for five years. And when I was a member of the gang, they weren't doing any of that stuff. The smoking, drinking and street violence were enough.

VIC   I don't believe you! The Kapps are the sworn enemies of The Montz! I . . . uh . . . must sit down . . .

SAM   Just get back into this car!

VIC   No!

SAM   Get back into this car or you'll end up dead like my cousin! He wouldn't listen either. Always the gang. Allegiance to the gang even when they let him down and left him on the roadside to die! After the 'Fortress' deal.

VIC   You were at the 'Fortress' deal?

SAM   Some big stupid fight that was. A load of kids – screaming and running around until someone threw the first stone . . . then the first punch. No reason behind it at all but mindless bigotry. And Kinsey got hit too hard . . . The police arrived to break it up and everyone ran for it. Except for me. I was with him when he died. That's when I changed. Started helping people instead of hurting them.

VIC   The Kapps started all this!

SAM   Aren't you listening to me?

VIC   (*the pain increasing*) I ain't gonna be helped by you or no Kapp. I'll wait . . . till someone else passes by . . .

SAM   And that's exactly what you'll get! A passer-by! For some reason, no-one round here wants to help a young thug like you who causes gang mayhem on the streets. Just me. So take it while you can.

VIC   (*weakening further*) You . . . are my . . . enemy.

SAM   Based on what? Answer me!

VIC   Something . . . something in the past.

SAM   Exactly. You don't know. You're gonna die for no reason!

VIC   (*rips off coat and throws it at Sam*) Here. Take this. I don't want to be infected . . . by it . . . (*Coughs and sinks onto the ground, becoming weaker.*)

SAM   I have no connection with that gang's past whatever it is.

VIC   We're all connected with the past. The violence. The vengeance. The blood . . .

SAM   (*looking at him with great sadness*) I'm aware of my past, but I'm not connected to it. At least, not to the point that it will stop me from breathing. I don't care that you are a Montz. Why do you care that I was a Kapp?

VIC   Leave me alone . . .

SAM   You cannot let yourself die over some historical background! Now matters. Not then. Life is important. Life is precious. Are you really going to let your life slip away from you because of some stupid prejudice? I'm a good person. Don't prejudge me for what I used to be. Judge me for who I am – this man in front of you who does not know you and has no war with you – judge me for who I am right now. Here. Let me help you . . . Please . . .

Caring

List of Characters

Mum

Matt (10)

Grandad

Pria (16)

Dad

Family home. Late afternoon. Matt is watching television. A pair of crutches are leaning up against the settee where he is sitting. He has muscular dystrophy, a muscular wasting disease. Mum enters with a drink for him.

MUM   (*putting drink on side*) Here you are, love . . . It's not too hot, so drink it now . . . Don't leave it till it gets cold.

MATT   (*irritated*) I'm watching this film.

MUM   Good, is it?

MATT   It's all right.

MUM   Do you want me to turn it over for you? . . . Only I think there are cartoons on the other side –

MATT   No! Leave it! I want to see this!

Enter Grandad, carrying a basket of clean washing off the line, who immediately defuses the situation.

GRANDAD   Oh, leave him alone, Margaret, for God's sake. I can hear you two from the garden. (*Puts the basket down by the ironing board in the corner then sits next to Matt.*)

MUM   Well, you make sure Matt drinks that before it goes cold. (*Exits.*)

GRANDAD   Fusses, doesn't she?

MATT	Too much.
GRANDAD	She means well.
MATT	She does my head in.
GRANDAD	She was fussy as a child. Just like her mother. It's congenital. In the blood.
MATT	So's a lot of stuff.

Grandad winces. He hadn't meant to refer to Matt's condition. Then he smiles at Matt.

GRANDAD	You're very smart for twelve.
MATT	I feel very old for twelve.
GRANDAD	(*Leans across and gives Matt a kiss.*) I love you very much, mate.
MATT	I know. (*Takes his grandad's hand.*)
GRANDAD	And your Mum's a pain in the nether regions, but we love her as well, don't we?
MATT	Yeah. I suppose so.
GRANDAD	You know, I think your grip's getting stronger, Matty.
MATT	(*smiling, resigned to his condition more than his grandad*) No, it's not.
GRANDAD	(*insistent*) Yes. It is.

Grandad kisses his hand, thinking how realistic Matt is being.

PRIA	(*entering, dressed up in a very short skirt ready to go out*) I'm off out now. (*Gives Matt a big kiss.*) See ya, Tiger.
MATT	Get off, Pria.
GRANDAD	That skirt's too short. You'll have all the lads after you.
PRIA	That's the idea.
GRANDAD	Seeing that Owen, are you?
PRIA	(*smiling very knowingly*) Sort of. In a way. I'll tell you about it later.

DAD (*getting in from work: offstage*) I'm home!

PRIA Oops. I am definitely out of here.

DAD (*enters and sees Pria's short skirt*) Off.

PRIA It's fashionable, Dad. (*Sits on armchair on the other side of Matt.*)

DAD Off, now. Never mind sitting down.

PRIA I'm doing my nails. I'll change in a minute. (*Whispers to Matt.*) When you've gone out.

MATT (*trying to drink*) I never go out.

GRANDAD (*seeing that Matt is getting worked up again*) Now then . . .

MATT I mean, why all this fuss about legs? At least Pria's work properly. What's the big deal about the length of her skirt? It's just a covering. At least they work! At least she can walk! (*Accidentally knocks drink over.*)

MUM (*rushing in*) What was that? Oh, now look. I'll get it. (*Tries mopping it up with a tissue.*) Was this you, Pria?

PRIA No, it wasn't.

MUM Get a cloth.

Pria exits to get a cloth.

MUM Not to worry, Matt.

MATT I'm fine.

MUM Why you have got to argue with Pria all the time, George, I don't know.

DAD We weren't arguing. I was telling her what she was going to do.

MATT Don't fuss, Mum, please. I hate it when you fuss. Grandad . . .

DAD I'll get you another drink.

MATT (*shouting*) Just leave me *alone*, will you!

Silence. No-one knows what to do now that Matt is this upset.

MATT   I'm going to my room. (*He uses his crutches and moves towards to the door.*)

MUM   Do you want me to –

GRANDAD   (*stopping her*) No. He doesn't.

Matt exits. Pria returns with cloth and mops floor.

MUM   It's managing the stair-lift. I can help –

GRANDAD   Let him manage on his own while he can.

PRIA   (*getting up*) I'm off.

DAD   Where you going?

PRIA   Out.

DAD   Now?

PRIA   What else is there to do?

DAD   You could stop in and talk to your brother, that's what!

PRIA   He doesn't *want* anyone to talk to him!

DAD   What have you done for him today? Nothing. As usual.

PRIA   Don't start.

DAD   Got him out of bed? Bathed him? Changed him?

PRIA   No. And neither did you. Mum did. Mum always does. You just escape out to work every day and leave her to it!

GRANDAD   That's enough, you two!

MUM   Stop all this rowing, can't you? You don't think what it does to other people.

DAD   She's selfish, Margaret, and she doesn't care – and I don't care who knows it.

PRIA   I'm not. I care about Matt. He's my brother. Of course I care! Don't you say I don't! I hate you!

Silence.

GRANDAD	*(calmly)* No-one hates anyone in this family. No-one. We all stick together. Because it's the only way we've got of coping with this. Take back what you said, Pria.
PRIA	But –
GRANDAD	Now.
PRIA	*(quietly)* I didn't mean it. *(Flops back down in the armchair.)*
GRANDAD	Son?
DAD	*(quietly)* I'm sorry. It was my fault. I started on you as soon as I walked in. I didn't mean to. It's just – I get my heart ripped out when I see Matt. Struggling with everything. Getting weaker by the day it seems sometimes. And I love him so much. And I can't do a thing to help him.
PRIA	*(goes to Dad and puts her arms round him)* You do. You and Mum and Grandad, you do everything you can for him. It's me. I go out all the time –
MUM	That's not true, love.
PRIA	It is, Mum. I can't cope.
MUM	You help us round the house and you tidy up and you shop. You talk to Matt all the time and you listen to him. You make him laugh. I wish I did. I seem to just wind him up these days.
GRANDAD	Margaret, if it weren't for you organising us and keeping us going, we'd have all gone under years ago, so stop it. And it's you who contacted the Muscular Dystrophy Association who've been so supportive. Plus the laptop for his schoolwork through that disability allowance scheme.
MUM	I fuss too much. It drives him mad. But I – it's as if – if I can just keep helping him, just keep him going, he might just pick up a bit. He might just not get any worse . . .

DAD   It's not chickenpox, Margaret. It's muscular dystrophy.

MUM   (*angry in her upset*) I know! Do you think I don't know? He's my child. He came out of my body. And this is the best I could do for him? Give him this sickly package of health?

DAD   It's not your fault, love.

PRIA   Mum, don't be daft.

MUM   It is. I've got this and now I've passed it on to Matt. His own mother! I'm supposed to nurture him, not destroy him! (*Cries.*) Why is he worse than me? Why? It's soul destroying!

DAD   (*leaving Pria and hugging Mum*) Margaret, there is no blame attached to any of this. It's just a biological lottery.

GRANDAD   I actually think he's a lot better now that special hydrotherapy treatment has started. I think he's a lot stronger.

MUM   Why? Why are we being punished like this?

DAD   It's not punishment. This is just the way it is for us. But at least he has us . . . and we've still got him. And I'll hang on to every second of that, I can tell you. He's here, with us. Breathing. I'll settle for that.

Pria moves across to the washing-basket and starts rummaging through it.

PRIA   Are these jeans all right to wear, Mum?

MUM   They're clean. Just washed today. They'll need ironing. Why?

PRIA   (*puts jeans on ironing board*) I'm wearing them for going out in. (*Gets out mobile and punches in a number.*)

DAD   Wear the skirt. I'm not bothered.

PRIA   (*smiling*) Not where I'm going. (*Into mobile.*) Hiya. It's me. I'm going to the pictures tonight with my brother.

Do you wanna come? . . . The revenge thing at Owen's party? . . . No, I can't be bothered with him. I'll just chuck a can of pop down his trousers tomorrow . . . Great. And bring Stefan . . . Yeah. See ya. (*Ends call.*)

GRANDAD   Is that young Stefan who's got about three million Game Boy discs in a big bag that he carries around with him?

PRIA   That's the one. (*Goes to door, opens it and calls up the stairs.*) Matt! Get down here now!

MATT   (*offstage*) No!

PRIA   (*very big sister*) Now, I said! We're going to the pictures!

MATT   I don't want to!

PRIA   Well, you'd better. Sean and Stefan will be here in a minute.

Silence.

PRIA   You deaf or something? Sort yourself out or we're going without you. (*Goes to ironing board and starts ironing jeans.*)

DAD   He won't go.

PRIA   He's got to.

GRANDAD   He will. He's strong. He's like his old grandad.

Silence. The family look expectantly in the direction of Matt's room.

MATT   (*offstage*) Mum! Where's my new T-shirt?

Marriage

List of Characters

Liz (17)

Nick (14)

Jack (17)

Helen, their mum

A roadside. A family's car has broken down. Helen, her two sons and Liz, her elder son Jack's girlfriend, are stranded, waiting for Helen's boyfriend to pick them up. Liz narrates to the audience and interacts with the other characters.

LIZ 'Let me not to the marriage of two minds admit impediments . . . ' (*To audience*) Although what else is there to do? Marriage is not an easy thing. There are going to be impediments. Like Jack.

HELEN Oh, stop pulling a face, Jack!

NICK Is the car going to blow up, we ask ourselves? Or just my big brother.

LIZ (*to audience*) We were all stranded on the side of the road, waiting for Helen's boyfriend to rescue us. From the cold. And from Jack.

JACK Well, I hope 'Fred' isn't going to take too long.

LIZ (*to audience*) Helen's fella was called James Flintly. Jack thought it had a nice caveman ring to it. (*To Jack*) Pack it in, Jack. It's cold and we don't want to hear it.

JACK You've lost that loving feeling then, Liz.

LIZ At the side of the road in the freezing cold? Yeah. I have.

JACK I'll have to trade you in for a new model.

LIZ	I'll have to rip out your windpipe and use it as a skipping-rope.
NICK	And a fight, too! Well worth being stranded and turning blue for.
JACK	Shut up, 'Barney'. (*Grabs Nick by the collar.*)
HELEN	Let him go, Jack!
JACK	I'm sick of him.
LIZ	And we're sick of you.
JACK	You're not even in this family, Liz, so you can shut up.
HELEN	Jack!
LIZ	Thank God! (*To audience*) Jack couldn't be unhappy on his own. He had to take hostages. (*To Jack*) That's the last time you're going to get the chance to say that to me. As soon as James gets here, I am out of your life for good. It's about time you grew up.
JACK	I don't need a behaviour talk from someone who got dragged off by the police.
LIZ	I was on an animal-rights protest and got dragged *out of the way* of the lab people as they arrived for work.
NICK	Well, I think it was really cool. Trying to change things.
LIZ	Your brother seems to think it was a riot.
HELEN	There'll be a riot in a minute. Where is he? He said he'd be twenty minutes.
JACK	I didn't know cavemen had watches. That's very hi-tech for what's-his-name.
HELEN	The man I'm going to marry is called James. It would be nice of you to remember it before the wedding.
JACK	(*darkly responsive*) Not in this lifetime.
HELEN	(*encouraging a confrontation*) As of next spring. A nice springtime wedding to blow the old cobwebs away.

LIZ   (*to audience*) Helen had had enough. She was up for a bit of mother–son bloodletting. And I'd had enough, too. (*Getting Nick back into the car.*) Why don't we listen to the radio in the car, Nick?

NICK   Oh. Okay. Is something wrong?

LIZ   Things are just a little like this car at the moment. Stalled.

Liz and Nick get into the car.

JACK   He's spineless and he's not coming into our house.

HELEN   My house. Your father left it to me.

JACK   To be passed on to me and Nick as next of kin. When did Flintly become successor to the throne?

HELEN   He's marrying me, not invading Poland! And you know the house is willed to you and Nick. Nothing's going to change that. You're my kids. You're your dad's kids. And nothing's going to change that either.

JACK   (*bitterly*) Apart from you.

LIZ   (*to audience*) To be honest, Nick was more fun to be with than Jack. The closer the wedding was getting, the more unbearable Jack was becoming.

NICK   Don't upset yourself over Jack, Liz. He's really not worth it. Was what you said outside just for show? About packing him in?

LIZ   What do you want to know for?

NICK   Just wondered. I don't see what his problem is with James. I think he's okay.

LIZ   He's smashing. He's really kind and he's always there for the family. (*To audience*) Though Jack would always put a negative slant on that.

JACK   He's just trying to get round us all the time.

HELEN   That's not true.

JACK	Pretending to be interested in us all the time. Taking us out and trying to help me with my coursework. Well, I don't need his help! As he soon found out!
HELEN	You dare swear at him again or slam the door in his face and you'll be off to your aunt's for a month. See how you like that!
JACK	I'd love it! A month out of the sight and stench of Flintly? I can't wait. And I'm not going to that stupid celebration night of his either!
HELEN	Good! I won't have to look at The Face!
LIZ	(*to audience*) The centenary celebrations. The hundred years of the town's official commitment to the arts. James was organising the catering.
JACK	He's a cook.
HELEN	He's an important caterer.
JACK	He bakes cakes and butters bread. He's practically a woman.
HELEN	Please! Did my twenty-first-century son just say that? More pathetic things you don't believe in just to find something else negative to say about James.
JACK	I hate him!
HELEN	I don't care!
JACK	You're married to Dad!
HELEN	Your dad's dead!

Jack looks very hurt very suddenly. He leans against the bonnet of the car, folding his arms more out of security than defence.

HELEN	(*gently, not wanting to hurt him*) Jack . . . life moves on.
JACK	(*hurt*) Not for me. How can you be married to two men? How can you stand in a church and say that you'll love Dad forever, then say it again to Flintly?

HELEN James. His name's James. I meant what I said to your father that day I married him. I will always love your father. I will never love anyone else like I loved him.

JACK Then you can't marry Flintly. Can't you just live with him?

HELEN No.

JACK Why not?

HELEN Because I know how I feel. I love James – not in the same way that I loved your father. That was unique. But I do love him and I want to settle down into a life with him. And Nick. And you.

JACK I'm last on the list, I see.

HELEN Stop twisting everything into a negative. You're just keeping your hate going. I'm trying to put a family together here.

JACK We're already a family. You and me and Nick.

HELEN No. That's *your* family. That's who *you* need. But I need James, too, and I want him to be part of the family. And Nick does.

LIZ (*to audience*) Nick was a lot more willing to get to know James. To see him as a person in his own right, not some home-wrecking villain.

NICK He's just a really ordinary bloke. We played basketball yesterday. He used to play for the area. Still runs a local youth team.

LIZ A sporty hero. Another notch for Jack's hate-post.

NICK I've got tickets for a game next week. Would you like to go with me?

LIZ That's so sweet, Nick . . . but wouldn't you rather take some girlfriend?

NICK You're a friend. You're a girl. I think that just about covers it.

LIZ	What about Jack?
NICK	I thought you'd packed him in.
LIZ	It's not as simple as that . . .
HELEN	(*to Jack*) I saw you yesterday. Watching James and Nick playing basketball.
JACK	(*defensively*) I wasn't.
HELEN	Your dad used to play basketball with you. Remember? He even bought you and him matching shirts to play in. What did he have printed on them?
JACK	(*smiling in spite of himself*) The Slam-Dunk Stealers.
HELEN	It was good then, wasn't it?
JACK	I loved playing basketball. I haven't played since.
HELEN	Then it's about time you did.
NICK	(*to Liz*) You're not going to marry Jack, are you?
LIZ	Marry Jack? No! It's just that . . . it's not over between us yet.
NICK	It sounded like it was. Why do you still want him? He's awful, he's rude, he's sulky like a child. . . If I were a girl, I wouldn't even look at him.
LIZ	I've known him for years. Since primary school. In a way, it's like a –
NICK	Marriage? Don't be so romantic over him, Liz.
LIZ	You're too young for me, Nick.
NICK	Three years!
JACK	(*to Helen, a lot calmer now*) It won't be the same.
HELEN	No, it won't. It won't be the same as it was with your dad. But then, I don't want it to be.
JACK	I just feel this bond with Dad . . .
HELEN	Me, too, Jack.
JACK	It's like . . .

HELEN A marriage. (*Trying to explain.*) Marriage, love . . . Written. Unwritten. It's still an agreement to love, honour and be faithful to each other. All of us.

JACK Till death us do part.

HELEN For now. Not forever. I need to make a new bond with someone. And so do you. It's the only way to live. So you can't shut yourself off, Jack.

JACK I don't know what else to do . . .

HELEN Open up and adapt. Talk more to Liz.

LIZ (*to audience*) I never really knew what Jack was thinking. He never let me in.

JACK Liz doesn't want to know me any more. Open heart or shut case.

HELEN It's not you. It's the act you're putting on.

LIZ (*to audience*) The mask of aggression. Every day was fixing it more in place.

HELEN Do something, Jack, before it's too late.

JACK (*thinks, then goes to the car*) Nick. Get out.

NICK We're talking.

JACK Out.

LIZ Please, Nick.

NICK (*getting out of the car*) He's not good enough for you.

Jack gets into the car with Liz. Nick joins Helen.

HELEN (*to Nick*) Stop making moves on your brother's girlfriend. Oh, look! At last! It's James. (*Waving*) James!

NICK Why do jerks like my brother get all the best women?

HELEN He hasn't got her. He'll be lucky if she sees him again.

NICK She said it wasn't over yet.

HELEN In her head it's not over. But what she thinks and what she actually does are two very different things.

NICK   Eh?

HELEN   Which is why she's too old for you.

They both exit.

LIZ   *(to audience)* Jack had the nerve to try the sorry-thing on me. The little-boy sorry. I let him have it. *(To Jack)* Sorry doesn't cover it! What about what you're doing to everyone's lives? Who knows what your anger could do to your mum's relationship with James? He's got to feel like he's needed. Like he belongs. Not just to his wife, but to her children. His children. Marriage goes deep. It redefines who you all are.

JACK   I wasn't expecting a psychology lecture.

LIZ   It's not a lecture! It's the truth. Your mum's going to marry that man whether you like it or not. Get used to it and start bonding with him. He's a really decent person. It shouldn't be too hard to do.

JACK   Have I lost you, Liz?

LIZ   I need a break from you, Jack. You're hard work. I'm going away for a couple of weeks. Part of the course I'm on, then I'm visiting relatives. I'll see you when I get back. See how things are then.

JACK   I do love you, you know, Liz. I mean, I don't say it much –

LIZ   You never say it, Jack.

JACK   But I do. I just wanted you to know.

LIZ   I know. *(Kisses him.)*

JACK   I'm just finding things difficult at the moment.

LIZ   You're making things difficult at the moment. Don't miss out on this. He's over there now. Speak to him.

Jack thinks about this, very unsure, then gets out of the car.

JACK   *(pauses, then calls out to James offstage)* Can I help you with that . . . James?

Mob

List of Characters

Teacher	Victim
Mob 1	Pleb 1
Mob 2	Pleb 2
Mob 3	Pleb 3
Mob 4	Pleb 4
Cinna	

NOTES:

If read and not performed, clearly Cinna and the four Plebs can be read by the same people reading for the Victim and the four Mob characters.

A split-scene – a classroom where Shakespeare's Julius Caesar is being taught, and a street where a victim is being set upon by a mob.

Classroom:

TEACHER *(talking to the group of actors)* In Act 3, Scene 3 of *Julius Caesar* we see Shakespeare's blueprint for mob violence. It happened then. It happens now.

Street:

MOB 1 There's nothing happening. I need a power fix.

Classroom:

TEACHER Caesar was dead. Mark Antony wanted to take over one of the now available seats of power. He spoke at Caesar's funeral and drove all the mindless plebeians – the poor people of the town – to burn down the

homes and kill all the conspirators who had
assassinated Caesar.

Street:

MOB 2 We need something to do. A cause. A purpose.

Classroom:

TEACHER Antony knew that the plebeians were easily swayed
to any way of thinking. Easily led. In their empty lives
of poverty and hardship, it was a cause, a meaning, a
chance to wield power. Antony used them to get the
job done. Who uses them now?

Street:

MOB 3 I heard on the news –

MOB 4 Read in the paper –

MOB 1 Heard on the radio –

MOB 2 Heard my mate say that there are killers on the loose
– or something.

MOB 3 Something -path. Bad people.

MOB 4 Something -path. Scum of the earth.

MOB 1 A better place without them.

MOB 2 A big campaign about it somewhere.

MOB 3 Heard it somewhere.

MOB 4 That'll do.

Classroom:

TEACHER That's what I need to see. The mob closing in on the
innocent victim for no good reason other than that
they have been given an excuse to. A cause. You kill
Cinna the poet, knowing ultimately that he is not
Cinna the conspirator, but revelling in the power that

you have been given by Antony. Do you understand?
Let me see this then.

*The actors form a semi-circle, facing the audience. The
mob stand in a mirror-image of them on the other side of
the acting space. Cinna and Victim enter into their
respective areas. Cinna has some poetry scrolls. Victim
has a briefcase.*

Classroom:

Plebeians surround Cinna.

PLEB 1   What is your name?

PLEB 2   Whither are you going?

PLEB 3   Where do you dwell?

PLEB 4   Are you a married man or a bachelor?

Street:

Mob surrounds Victim.

MOB 1   What's *your* name then?

MOB 2   Where you off to, eh?

MOB 3   Where you from, mate?

MOB 4   Got the girlfriend with you?

Classroom:

TEACHER   Now you've got him scared. Boom your power
at him!

ALL PLEBS   Answer every man directly!

Street:

ALL MOB   I'm talking to you!

Classroom:

TEACHER Now start pushing him about a bit. Can you feel his fear? Can you feel how good it is to make someone feel that frightened?

CINNA I am going to Caesar's funeral.

Street:

VICTIM I'm off to work. My car's just over there.

Classroom:

Plebeians start pushing Cinna around from one to another.

PLEB 1 As a friend or an enemy?

CINNA As a friend.

Street:

MOB 1 Got a nice car have you?

VICTIM It's all right.

Classroom:

PLEB 2 That matter is answered directly.

Both Cinna and Victim are hit simultaneously and both fall to the ground.

Classroom:

TEACHER Grab him by his collar! By his hair! Make him answer you! This is your moment of power!

PLEB 4 (*grabbing Cinna*) For your dwelling, briefly!

CINNA Briefly, I dwell by the Capitol!

Street:

MOB 2 (*doing the same to Victim*) Where you going?

MOB 3 Answer me!

| MOB 4 | Quick! |
| VICTIM | In town! I work in an office in town! |

Classroom:

| TEACHER | All of you, close in! Make him tell you who he is! Make him feel small and answerable to *you*! |
| PLEB 3 | Your name, sir, truly! |

Street:

| MOB 1 | Your name! What's your *name*? |

Classroom:

| CINNA | Truly, my name is Cinna! |

Street:

| VICTIM | I'm not telling you *anything*! |

Mob 1 raises his fist to Victim.

MOB 2	(*going through his jacket pocket and finding a business card*) Hello. What have we here? A business card. With a *name* on it!
MOB 3	What does it say? Scum?
MOB 4	Traitor?
MOB 1	Enemy?
MOB 2	It says 'Sean Sinden: Homeopath'.
MOB 3	Something -path.
MOB 4	Something *-path*!

Classroom:

| TEACHER | You have your answer! That's all you've been waiting for! Attack! |
| PLEB 1 | Tear him to pieces, he's a conspirator! |

CINNA   I am Cinna the poet, I am Cinna the poet!

PLEB 4   Tear him for his bad verses, tear him for his bad verses!

CINNA   I am not Cinna the conspirator!

Street:

MOB 1   Tear him apart!

MOB 2   Homeopath!

MOB 3   Scum of the earth!

MOB 4   Enemy of the people!

VICTIM   No! I'm a homeopath! I deal in complementary medicine. I treat people's illnesses with minute doses of natural substances – extracts from flowers and plants.

Classroom:

TEACHER You don't want to listen to that! You don't want to let him go. He is your victim. Hurting him makes you feel powerful. Makes you feel strong! Kill him!

PLEB 4   It is no matter . . .

Street:

MOB 1   It doesn't matter . . .

Classroom:

PLEB 4   His *name's* Cinna.

Street:

MOB 1   Your *name's* close enough. Something -path. Homeopath. Close enough.

MOB 2   Tear him up!

MOB 3   Rip his heart out!

Classroom:

PLEB 4 Pluck but his name out of his heart, and turn him going!

PLEB 3 Tear him, tear him!

The Plebeians and the Mob drag Cinna and the Victim off stage simultaneously. We hear a struggle, screams of pain and then silence.

The Plebians and the Mob regroup onstage, pumped with energy and rage.

Classroom:

TEACHER Feel that lust of the blood! The power! You want to kill again. Find another victim! As it was, so shall it be again!

PLEB 3 Come, brands, ho!

MOB 4 Fire brands!

PLEB 1 To Brutus's!

MOB 1 To Cassius's!

PLEB 2 Burn all!

MOB 2 Some to Decius's house!

PLEB 3 And some to Casca's!

MOB 3 Some to Ligarius's!

ALL PLEBS ⎫
ALL MOB ⎭ Away, go!

All the Plebeians and Mob exit shouting and laughing in a frenzied desire to find more victims.

TEACHER (*stepping forward to address the audience – seriously, warningly, a chilling final statement*) Now let it work. Mischief, thou art afoot. Take thou what course thou wilt.

Bond

List of Characters

Woman

Pool Director 1

Pool Director 2

Pool Director 3

The future. Woman sitting in a chair within a spotlight, having arrived for her appointment with the Pool Directors of 'The Gene Pool', a manufacturing and storage facility for babies. 'The Gene Pool' has replaced the need for women to have babies themselves. All birth is controlled now. People wishing to have a baby must apply for one to be 'Arranged'.

PD1   Do sit down, please. Do we have all your information?

WOMAN   Thank you. Yes, you do. I gave my disk in to the Dispatch Officer.

PD3   Everything's in order on the information screen. What can we do for you?

WOMAN   I want to have a baby.

PD1   Of course.

PD2   What sex and colour did you have in mind?

PD3   As you know, twins may not be allocated until next season.

PD1   Due to an unusual demand for them in the last twelve months.

PD2   Birth trends. . .We have to keep a balance within the system.

PD3   But any form of single issue is acceptable.

PD1   Intelligence requirements A to E?

PD2   Athletic ability Z1 to Z5?

PD3   Any talents required to be specified now and to be programmed into the Arrangement in the last two months before Delivery.

WOMAN   No. You don't understand. I want the baby.

PD1   *You* do?

WOMAN   I don't want it Arranged. I want it naturally. I have a partner.

PD3   Personal donors are not allowed.

PD1   All Arrangements are under the strict control of The Gene Pool.

PD2   The Gene Pool has its own bank of donations.

PD3   All highly scrutinised, tested and processed to remove all contamination.

PD3   Disease.

PD1   Abnormalities.

PD2   All Arrangements Delivered via The Gene Pool are healthy.

PD3   And one hundred per cent fully functional.

WOMAN   And anonymous. My husband and I want our own baby. I have included on the disk our medical records and, as you can see, there is no record of major illness in either of our families. Our child, therefore, can only be healthy.

PD1   You cannot rely on Nature to produce a healthy Arrangement.

PD2   Only Science can do that.

PD3   Science provides perfection.

WOMAN   We want our own child. I want to give birth to *my* child, not to the contents of some vacuum-sealed kit!

PD1   Please do not make light of this situation.

WOMAN   I'm not, I *assure* you.

PD2 Personal Arrangements are not allowed any more by *law*.

PD3 To help eradicate political upheaval and social disturbance in the world, fifty years ago The Gene Pool was established –

WOMAN I *am* aware of recent social history . . .

PD1 The Gene Pool was established to make sure that only healthy and socially stable Arrangements were given access to the system.

WOMAN Allowed to be born, you mean.

PD2 You must see the reasoning behind these requirements.

WOMAN No. I don't.

PD3 Due to the processing work of The Gene Pool, no Arrangement is Delivered into the system that has any genetic deficiency.

PD1 Or emotional instability.

PD2 Physical abnormality.

WOMAN Or individuality.

PD3 And because the Unit the Arrangement is Delivered to has no prior connection to it, there are no physical or emotional similarities or unwanted alignments.

WOMAN Alignments?

PD1 People can become extraordinarily aggressive and disturbed should a baby look like someone in particular, or remind them of someone in particular, or be of a certain gender, or be the result of some relationship now terminated . . .

PD2 Humans are messy creatures.

WOMAN You're not human then?

PD3 The Gene Pool is here to provide society with healthy, stable and functioning material with an absence of dysfunctional extremists.

WOMAN	I disagree!
PD1	The Gene Pool is creating Utopia!
WOMAN	The Gene Pool is creating hell! What kind of a world is this when people are no longer acceptable if 'imperfect'? Where everyone is the same passive and dismally unresponsive person as everyone else?
PD2	This meeting is terminated.
WOMAN	We were all created differently for a *purpose*!
PD3	Not any more.
WOMAN	Our different skills, backgrounds, cultures, features, abilities made for a more creative world!
PD1	And a more violent society!
WOMAN	Individuality does not create violence! Oppression does! Like being 'invented' by The Gene Pool! Being told that we cannot have our own children, establish our own lives and exercise our own free will!
PD2	Your disk is being returned to you as being insubmissible.
WOMAN	Frankenstein's monster was created with more love and consideration than this!
PD3	Please remove your disk from Slot C on the right-hand side of the control panel in front of you.
WOMAN	You create to control! This isn't Science assisting Nature like with IVF. This is Science playing God!
PD1	Please remove your disk.
WOMAN	I want my own child!
PD2	Please remove your disk.
WOMAN	I demand the right to give birth to my own child!
PD2	Please remove your *disk*!
WOMAN	I will *not* be dictated to!

Interest
List of Characters

Two characters with no names

NOTES:

What makes for a lasting friendship? Can people be friends yet have very little in common? What keeps them together?

A   Why are we such good friends? After all these years?

B   Shared interests?

A   Not really. Do you like basketball, swimming and fishing?

B   No. I hate fishing. I don't know why you do it.

A   Neither do I. You used to come fishing with me.

B   I wanted to be with you. I thought that if you liked fishing, I might grow to like it too.

A   And did you?

B   No. I hate fishing.

A   I never could see what you liked about bowling. Knocking down skittles.

B   Pins.

A   Just to have some machine put them back up again. Very irritating.

B   Like spending three hours sitting on a damp riverbank to catch a fish, only to let it go again.

A   Three hours? Five!

B   Do we like the same food and drink?

A   Not really. You're all salads and fresh food and I do so like frozen pies and the chilled-food cabinet of processed delights.

B   That's why I look younger than you.

A   Says who?

B   Films and telly. We watch the same stuff. Oh, but those Westerns and Romances you like!

A   You watch too many of those rough-stuff crime films. You'll probably turn into a gangster one day. Shame me by going around robbing banks.

B   Do we like the same people?

BOTH   No!

A   Spare me from some of your friends! Sheila with the hysterical laugh.

B   What about your friend Will with all the jokes that never have any punch-lines?

A   He thinks they do. We have to humour him. He's affected by the moon, you know.

B   Is that why he falls down such a lot outside pubs at night?

A   Tragic, isn't it?

B   Have we got anything in common?

A   Er . . .

B   Well?

A   Er . . . Each other. We both like each other.

B   It's my dazzling personality, isn't it?

A   It is, actually. Well, 'dazzling' is going a bit too far, but it is you – your humour and gentle understanding – that I like.

B   I like your knees.

A   Oh, shut up.

B   We're not joined at the hip, but we are emotionally inseparable. And we know when to give each other some space to have our own interests, yet share each other's lives.

A I couldn't imagine being without you.

B That's why I married you.

Listening

List of Characters

Four characters with no names

NOTES:

What does it feel like when no-one is listening? Why is it important that they should?

A (*to B*) Can I talk to you for a second?

B Oh, not now. Can't you see I'm busy?

A (*to B*) It won't take a minute.

C Get out the way, will ya? I can't see the telly with your Rear Of The Year in the way!

A (*to B*) This is important.

D Has anyone seen my work folder?

C Oh, great. There's *two* of them now!

B It's where you put it last.

D I don't *remember* where I put it last!

B Too bad. I'm not here to remember things for you. Lay the table.

D I'm busy!

A (*to B*) I just need to talk to you for a second. It's a bit sensitive.

B What is it? Turn that thing down!

C It's not up loud.

B Down or off. One or the other.

C I'll put the headphones on. Where are the headphones? Oh, great!

D Hey! There's my folder! Who's left this disgusting half-eaten sandwich on it?

C You probably.

D You more like.

A (*to B*) Please.

B What? I'm listening.

A No, you're not. You keep doing other things.

B I'm busy.

A But I need to talk to you in private. Now.

C You will *not* use my work folder as a plate!

D I didn't! I am being accused when I am innocent!

A (*to B*) It's really urgent.

B Go on then.

A Not in front of those two.

B Oh, for goodness' sake!

C You're *never* innocent!

D I protest. (*Grabbing A.*) Come here, you.

A Ow! Get off. I don't want to listen to all your mad stuff.

D Did you see me eating a sandwich in here today? No. Thank you.

C She didn't say anything!

D She did. She shook her head.

C You nudged her!

A Won't anyone listen to me?

B Oh, shut up, you two. Nobody wants to hear about some old sandwich!

A This is important!

C I'm fed up of people messing up my stuff!

A I'm fed up of people ignoring me!

D I'm fed up of being blamed for everything!

A I've started my period!

Section 3:
Healthy, Safer Lifestyles
Scripts for the Body

Travel

List of Characters

Dad
Mum
Martin
Ronny
Richie

A family is packing, getting ready to go on holiday. Dad is searching for something, his suitcase open on the floor.

MUM **(***enters with clothes***)** Pants, socks, shirts, T-shirts. Here. **(***Hands dad clothes, all folded. When ignored.***)** Here!

DAD **(***looking for something***)** What?

MUM Clothes. Or are you going to wear what you've got on for the entire holiday and smell?

DAD I never smell, darling. Stink, yes. Smell, never. **(***Takes clothes.***)** The baby smells.

MUM The baby! I must stuff a few more things into your suitcase for her. **(***Continues talking as she exits.***)** Ronny! Bring the baby down. It's time for her feed.

RONNY **(***offstage***)** Okay! Anyone seen my 'Shameless Hussy' T-shirt?

MUM **(***offstage***)** You are *not* wearing that on holiday!

RONNY **(***offstage***)** Why not?

MUM **(***offstage***)** *No!* **(***Re-enters with more clothes.***)** Baby clothes, baby-mat, pants. What *are* you looking for?

DAD The corkscrew.

MUM That's hardly important, is it?

DAD I go nowhere without it.

MUM   They'll sell there there.

DAD   More buying? Certainly not.

MUM   Did you pack the first-aid kit?

DAD   Yes. For the tenth time.

MUM   I'm sorry, sweetheart, but it's important. You never know what might happen.

MARTIN   (*entering*) Did anyone remember to pack the first-aid kit?

DAD   Yes!

MARTIN   Here. Extra plasters, bandages, wasp-sting ointment and stuff for mosquitoes.

MUM   Good thinking. Mosquitoes. Forgot about them. Where's the mosquito-net? (*Exits.*)

DAD   I can't get any more into this case!

MARTIN   You're not doing it right. You're wasting too much space. There's an art to packing a suitcase.

DAD   Don't tell me how to pack. I've been packing suitcases for years, *well* before you were born, thank you.

RONNY   (*entering with baby*) Din-dins? Is it? Is it din-dins time for you? Is it? Yes, it is, isn't it? It's din-dins time for Baby!

MARTIN   Shut it Ronny. You sound mental.

RONNY   Shut it yourself, Martin. (*To Baby*) It's nasty old Martin, isn't it? With his nasty old squitty prawn-face, isn't it?

MARTIN   Why do you keep asking it questions? What would you do if it answered you? Eh?

RONNY   *She* does answer me, Martin, and makes more intelligent conversation than *you*.

MARTIN   (*tickling baby*) Ronny's crackers, isn't she, Babe? Yeah. Shall we lock her up in the shed? Shall we? (*To Ronny*) She said yes.

RONNY	No, she didn't. Here's the water purifier, Dad, in case the water's grotty.
DAD	Oh, give it here!
MUM	(*entering with more things*) Bath-towels, hand-towels, tea-towels and pants.
DAD	More pants? I've got pants. I don't want any more pants. I've got enough to start a shop already.
RICHIE	(*entering*) Okay, I've been on the internet and checked the place out. No problems like curfews or restricted access to certain places due to political problems. No civil unrest or military presence on the streets – so no danger of riots, shootings and so forth. However, I still say we take the self-defence stuff, just in case. Sprays, stun-weapons . . .
DAD	Not in *my* case, you're not.
MARTIN	No, that stuff is hand luggage.
RICHIE	It's all hand luggage. I mean, why do we say hand luggage when *all* the cases have got handles?
MARTIN	(*sarcastically*) He's deep, isn't he?
RICHIE	Did anyone pack the first-aid kit?
DAD	Give me strength. Yes!
RICHIE	Only it's very important when travelling to be prepared.
DAD	You don't say.
RICHIE	I *do* say.
DAD	Fancy. And what else do you say, Richie?
RICHIE	Well, we've got to remember to make room for food.
DAD	Really?
RICHIE	When we get there, there might be a drought and ensuing food shortages.
DAD	Food shortages.

RONNY   Or there might be something eco-unfriendly like a plague of locusts which might have eaten all the food before we get there.

DAD   A plague of locusts! Of course! Why didn't I think of that?

MARTIN   This is something we haven't checked for yet. Richie, get back onto the internet and find out about the local diet, too.

DAD   Why?

MARTIN   Well, they might eat alligators, which I would have a spiritual, moral, not to mention biological dilemma with.

RONNY   Alligator! Oo! Baby couldn't eat elephant, could you? No, you couldn't. Not unless we take a turbo-charged blender with us.

DAD   Have I entered into a parallel universe and not been aware of it?

MARTIN   I mean, would the universe support me in doing this? Would it be right to do this? And could I actually digest an alligator?

RICHIE   He's deep, isn't he?

MUM   (*entering with more clothes*) Did anyone check for flood warnings and are we taking the inflatable life-raft?

DAD   That's it! Stop! (*To Richie, as he goes to exit.*) Freeze!

RICHIE   But the internet!

DAD   *Freeze!* (*To Mum, pointing at the pile of clothes in her arms.*) Are those pants?

MUM   No.

DAD   Are they?

MUM   They might be.

DAD   No!

MUM	But we use a lot of them.

DAD *(tiredly)* Sit down, everybody, please. (**As they hesitate.**) Please.

Everyone sits

DAD Now I know we're all trying to be very twenty-first century and organised in our forward thinking, but I think we're getting a wee bit over-cautious and, dare I say, manic? I can accept that we need to take precautions and take certain things, like stuff for the baby . . .

RONNY And the first-aid kit.

DAD Quite. But some of the other things are just *too* excessive. For example, Ronny. What is that bundle you have left by the door?

RONNY An inflatable guard-dog.

DAD And what would that be for?

RONNY If the place is too dangerous, we could sit him by the hotel door and people would think he was real enough to attack them. Especially as he has his own accompanying growling-and-barking tape. It's very clever. It just fits inside his tummy.

DAD Does it, indeed?

RONNY And we do have the baby to think of.

DAD We certainly do. And Martin, what do you have in that very long kit bag over there?

MARTIN I need them.

DAD What are they?

MARTIN They're essential travel-kit.

DAD What are they?

MARTIN Stilts.

DAD Stilts. For . . . ?

MARTIN   For the altitude. If it's too many miles above sea level, the air gets thinner down below, so you need stilts to get to the oxygen.

DAD   Eh? What are you on about?

RICHIE   Isn't that right?

DAD   No, it isn't! We're going on holiday. We are *not* going to war. You're all over-reacting. *And* – now listen, because this is very important – (*Quietly emphatic.*) We're going to *Devon*.

Silence.

RONNY   We won't be needing the inflatable nuclear fall-out and typhoon-warning bunker, then?

Smoke-Screen

List of Characters

PJ

Gav

Jat

Immy

Four pupils working on a piece for Drama.

PJ I don't agree.

GAV PJ!

JAT We can't keep stopping like this, man.

IMMY We've got to put together a piece about smoking and you're not making this any easier, PJ, by stopping all the time.

PJ What we're putting together is sappy and dismal. It's not hard-hitting enough.

GAV I'm not listening to this. We've got a deadline for the end of the lesson and this will do.

JAT Yeah. We're using the research, aren't we?

IMMY Let's just get on with it. Right, Gav – you're the dad and you've just found a packet of fags in my coat pocket when you were tidying up. Okay. Action.

GAV What are these?

IMMY What are you doing in my room?

GAV Tidying up after you. What are these?

IMMY I don't know, do I?

GAV Fags! How long have you been smoking fags?

IMMY I'm not smoking fags!

GAV	Don't lie to me! Wait till I tell your mum!
PJ	Urgh!
GAV	What?
PJ	What's this got to do with smoking? This is about disobeying your parents.
JAT	It's just the introduction. You've got to have a lead-in to the main action. Right. So I'm the mum. And in I come. Action. Hey! What's all this shouting about?
GAV	Your daughter's been smoking in secret!
JAT	*My* daughter? When did she stop being *your* daughter, too?
IMMY	Please, just stop all this rowing, will you? You're always rowing and I can't take it any more!
PJ	Urgh!
JAT	What?
PJ	Well, *now* it's just a domestic drama!
GAV	We're building up to it!
PJ	Up to what? A soap opera punch-up between these three? Don't tell me. The mum and dad have a massive row and blame each other for smoking in front of the daughter –
JAT	Yeah, well, that's using the research. That when both the parents smoke, the teenage child is more likely to smoke too than some other teenager who belongs to a family where neither parent smokes.
IMMY	You're assuming a family is made up of two parents.
PJ	Well, that's another point, isn't it? Why does our play have a mum and a dad? The family unit is made up of all sorts of different combinations of adults and children now.
IMMY	So we need to change the characters, then?
JAT	Oh, don't side with PJ, please! We'll be here all day!
GAV	We won't. The teacher will just go spare at us.

PJ We were working on this in yesterday's lesson, too, and you lot were messing about.

JAT I wasn't. It was those two. I was helping get research information off the internet, I was.

IMMY Wait a minute! That's not true!

PJ The point is, this play is no good. We're not using the research.

GAV We are! The smoking parents stuff, and then Immy's character runs off to see her friend – that's you – and she gets a fag out to smoke in front of you for her nerves or something.

JAT Yeah. Then you try and stop her from smoking in front of you by running off some of these other research details.

PJ Which I've just been studying in class for a project on smoking.

JAT (*in the tone of 'That's right'*) Yeah.

PJ (*same tone of voice*) No.

GAV Why not?

PJ Smoking is a *really* serious subject.

IMMY We know!

PJ I haven't finished yet. It's a really serious subject, so we can't just do a quick soap opera, then bung a few facts in at the end about how smoking is hazardous to health.

IMMY Soap operas are really effective, actually, for reporting on vital social issues. The programme makers have to research issues thoroughly before tackling them to be as informative and effective as possible.

JAT Charles Dickens used the press, like soap operas use the telly now, to promote the need for social change through his work. Got the law changed too, so don't down-grade soap operas.

PJ   Yeah? Well, our sad play is being neither.

GAV   There's too much to cover.

JAT   Look at all this stuff. The increase in SIDS due to passive smoking.

GAV   What's SIDS?

JAT   Sudden Infant Death Syndrome. That's babies dying. Cot deaths.

IMMY   Then there's all the smoking-related diseases and problems – lung cancer, heart disease, emphysema, asthma, smaller babies, premature birth . . .

GAV   What about this Health and Safety at Work Act from 1974? It stated that employers had to ensure the health, safety and welfare of their employees as far as was reasonably practical.

IMMY   Let's have a look . . . Oh, right, and then there was the amendment to that in 1993 when they had to provide rest-areas for employees which were non-smoking areas.

PJ   Then there's all the information about sidestream and mainstream smoke. Sidestream directly from the tip of the lit cigarette and mainstream which is the exhaled smoke. There's more toxic chemicals and gases in the sidestream smoke.

JAT   Four thousand different types.

GAV   And all the stuff off people's lungs in the mainstream? Gross!

IMMY   So what do we do then?

PJ   We've got to do spotlights. Each of us be a character who has suffered in some way from smoking or somebody else's smoking.

IMMY   A mother with a damaged baby.

GAV   An employee working in a place that is not following Health and Safety guidelines.

JAT A smoker who is suffering from a smoking-related disease.

PJ And someone about to take up smoking from peer-group pressure.

GAV What about the deadline?

IMMY We're not gonna make the deadline.

PJ We'll have to see Sir. The old play is a load of tat. The new one has something to say. We've got to start again.

Pressure

List of Characters

Ingram

Knox

Naylor

Teacher 1

Teacher 2

Split-scene – pupils standing at the bottom of a stairwell in a school, and a staffroom where teachers are talking about them.

Stairwell:

INGRAM My dad'll kill me.

KNOX Oh! You wimp! There's money in it! Money!

INGRAM I couldn't. Breaking and entering? It's criminal. I'll go to prison.

KNOX You are so stupid. You're too young to go to prison. They'll just give you a warning. In and out the station in five minutes.

Staffroom:

T1 Knox is after Ingram.

T2 Have you done your reports yet?

T1 I wish I taught Knox. I know what I'd put on *that* report.

T2 Ingram is weak. Everyone knows that.

T1 Only in the ability to say no.

T2 That's weak enough.

Stairwell:

KNOX What do you say? Eh?

INGRAM I don't know. The last time I got into trouble, I got such a belting. My dad said if I ever got into any more trouble, that'd be it.

KNOX He can't tell you what to do now. You're twelve. You want to stand up to him.

INGRAM What? To my dad? You're tapped, you are.

KNOX Think of the money. Stuff to be taken for the asking. And the gang. You'd be in the gang if you did it. One of the lads.

INGRAM How can I be one of the lads when I'm a girl?

Staffroom:

T1 I offered her a part in the school production and she wouldn't take it. Said she was too shy.

T2 But not too shy to hang around with Rat-Boy Knox and break into houses.

T1 She's unloved.

T2 Who isn't?

T1 Well, there's a reason why you're not.

T2 Thanks. Poor kid. Brutal father. Weak family. The only recognition she gets, I suppose, is from Knox.

T1 She's got no-one to turn to, she thinks.

Stairwell:

KNOX You're special.

INGRAM Am I?

KNOX You're brilliant at getting in and out of houses to let us in. Tight spaces that would be impossible for us. But not for you. It's a real talent.

Staffroom:

T2   What? She can't!

T1   I'm telling you, Ingram crawled through some dog-flap into a property for a dare, then let the rest of them in through the front door.

T2   Never!

T1   I talked to her anyway and warned her about Knox, getting in with that crowd.

T2   And she wasn't listening.

T1   Oh, she was listening, all right. She just won't accept that Knox will lead her into trouble as Knox is all she's got.

T2   She needs a friend.

Stairwell:

KNOX   You're really brilliant. And your dad? I tell mine where to get off and nothing comes of it.

NAYLOR   (*entering*) That's 'cause he's not listening to you, Knox.

KNOX   Oh, look who it isn't. Been sucking up to the teachers again, Naylor?

NAYLOR   I've been in detention. What you hanging around here for, Deana?

KNOX   Detention for what?

NAYLOR   Threatening a little nobody like you, Knox. Push off and mind your own business.

KNOX   You should have been suspended for that. Anyone else would have been, but the teachers favour you.

NAYLOR   The teachers probably had sympathy for me 'cause *they'd* have loved to have knocked Willis into the machine as well. 'Cause he's like *you*.

KNOX   We were having a private conversation.

NAYLOR   Oh, were you, Knox? I didn't know you could actually communicate properly without a grunt. Deana's feeding you some pig-swill to keep the chat going, is she?

KNOX   You're gonna get battered, Naylor. I'm gonna get me mates onto you.

NAYLOR   Me and my brothers battered your mates last time they tried to start it with us, and you know it. Still hiding behind your mates – *well* behind your mates – so that they can fight your battles for you? And, in return, I'll bet you do little jobs for them, like trying to rope Deana into something. Was that the little job they gave you today, Rat-Boy Gopher? Ah! Good dog. Come here and let me pat your head with me fist.

KNOX   Don't you touch me! I'll catch you later, Ingram. (*Exits.*)

Staffroom:

T1   I think she talks to Carl Naylor.

T2   In Year 9? I like him. He's hard.

T1   His 'hard' attitude is going to get him kicked out if he's not careful. He rammed Joe Willis into the can machine on Monday.

T2   I wondered what he was out for.

T1   I had a big word with him. Threatened to drop him from the school production?

T2   I'll bet you did.

T1   I said to him, 'Carl,' I said, 'if Joe Willis wants a fight with you in school, don't you *dare* take him up on it.' I told him to walk away, see me, see the Deputy, the Head, any of the staff and report it. Let the school deal with it. I told him to use the system and stop taking matters into his own hands.

T2	He should use Turnstiles. That's what it's there for with all the school volunteers and mentors for pupils to talk to. But he won't. Kids like Deana Ingram and Carl Naylor won't use it unless you force them to. They feel comfortable with the way they are. They like that feeling of power and danger juggling with dynamite.
T1	Until it blows up in their faces.
T2	Bottom line is, kids like their own way and some of them think we're the enemy.
T1	Why don't they ever think of the consequences of their actions?
T2	These reports are late for Mrs Francis. I need a go-between. You get on well with her. Couldn't you sort of run into her room with them, dump them on her table and tell her that you found them? In her pigeon-hole. Two days ago. They'd fallen out and you'd picked them up and forgotten to put them back in again.
T1	No.
T2	Some help you are.
T1	Try Turnstiles.

Stairwell:

NAYLOR	Try Turnstiles.
INGRAM	I can't tell people about me. Who'd care? And anyway, they'd just get me into loads of trouble.
NAYLOR	You stick with Knox and house-breaking. No trouble attached to that at all, is there?
INGRAM	Did Miss Sullivan send you to talk to me? She keeps on at me.
NAYLOR	No. You gonna be in the school production?
INGRAM	No.

NAYLOR Pity. It's good fun. I'm excellent in it.

INGRAM Don't think much of yourself, do you?

NAYLOR I respect myself enough not to hang around with Rat-Boy Knox. He doesn't like you, you know. He's using you. And his way leads nowhere. You're only Year 7. Don't get chucked out before you get to Year 8.

INGRAM I want something better for myself. I need to talk to someone. I can't talk to anyone at home, you see. No-one'd listen. But I don't want to settle for the life I've got . . . and I've got a terrible feeling I'm going the same way as my mum and my eldest sister. They both got married before they were twenty and they're both miserable. Trapped.

NAYLOR Well, try that Turnstiles thing, then! Make a decision.

INGRAM I'll go if you go.

Silence.

NAYLOR This isn't about me. It's about you.

Staffroom:

T1 I'm off to rehearsals now. They've all had plenty of time for toilets and eating their own body-weight in chocolate. See you later.

T2 What about these reports? What about Mrs Francis?

T1 Go and have a chat with her and work something out.

T2 I suppose I'd better brave up to it. (*Practising.*) Gwen! How lovely you look today! Like the boots. Just found these reports. Must have fallen out of your pigeon-hole . . .

Stairwell:

INGRAM Will you?

NAYLOR I'll think about it.

INGRAM	Tomorrow? It's really important.
NAYLOR	(*pausing*) I'll walk you up there. But you've got to come to rehearsals now. Let's go.
INGRAM	What, now?
NAYLOR	Phone home and tell them you're staying on for a while.
INGRAM	What about Knox? He'll be waiting for me at the gates.
NAYLOR	We'll tell Sullivan. Use the system. Focus on it. You'll be all right.
INGRAM	(*as they move off*) What happened with you and Joe Willis, then?
NAYLOR	Ah. A momentary lack of concentration . . .

Gross!

List of Characters

Shell ⎫
Lynz ⎬ Girls
Saj ⎭

Rob ⎫
Rav ⎬ Boys

A classroom, early morning, pre-registration. Puberty has struck everyone overnight. Completely! One by one, the pupils enter in various emotional states.

SHELL (*entering*) Lynz, you've got to come in.

LYNZ Everyone'll see me!

SHELL What are you gonna do? Stand in the corridor all day with your coat on?

LYNZ I can tell everyone I've got a cold and I don't want them to catch it.

SHELL Get in here!

LYNZ (*entering*) It's all right for you. You've just got spots.

SHELL Spots? Spots? Look at these things! It's a plague. A pestilence! Moses didn't dump stuff like this on the Egyptians! They just had a plague of frogs. I'd have no problem with a plague of frogs. I'd settle for that. I could just scurry around and put them in aerated jamjars and not have to spend a fortune on lotion.

LYNZ At least I've been spared them.

SHELL Thanks, Lynz! Right! That coat's coming off for that.

LYNZ (*hanging on to her coat*) No! I'm sorry! I didn't mean it!

SHELL Who's gonna want to date me now?

LYNZ Ah, Shell . . .

SHELL Tim won't.

LYNZ Ah, Shell . . .

SHELL The best-looking lad in the year. And the nicest. I've been working on him for ages to notice me, as well.

LYNZ Well, he'll certainly notice you now. No! Not the coat! Get your hands off me pegs!

SHELL Where *did* you get this duffle-coat from anyway?

LYNZ It's me dad's. He used to wear it at university.

SHELL What does that badge say? 'Ban . . . ' what?

LYNZ 'Fascist Multi-Nationals', Dad said.

SHELL And the other one?

LYNZ 'Ban Cream-Crackers'.

SHELL Not such a powerful message really. What you wearing it for?

LYNZ It's the only thing I could get on.

SHELL Why? What's up with you?

LYNZ Look. (*Opens her coat.*)

SHELL Yikes, Lynz! Fully stacked, or what?

LYNZ I hate them. Look at the size of them. Yesterday, I was wearing a Double A and I could hardly fill it. Today – Double D!

SHELL You might fall over.

LYNZ I'm trying not to.

SHELL Where'd you get the bra from?

LYNZ It's me nan's. Mum's wasn't big enough. I hate them. What's everyone gonna say? And my emotions! They're all over the place. I want to laugh and cry hysterically at the same time.

SHELL	That's not puberty. You were always like that.

SHELL That's not puberty. You were always like that.

LYNZ Oh.

SHELL And have you started . . . ?

LYNZ Yes.

SHELL I mean, I knew it was on the cards, but . . .

LYNZ It's gross.

SHELL I thought this stuff was supposed to happen gradually.

LYNZ I've always said they put hormones in the oven-ready chickens now.

BOTH (*hearing footsteps*) Oh no! Someone's coming!

LYNZ I'm doing me coat up again!

SHELL It's all right for some. Quick. We'll hide up the corner. Maybe no-one'll see us. Get your magazine out. We'll pretend to be totally engrossed in it and they won't bother us.

ROB (*entering*) Rav, you're gonna have to talk to me sometime.

RAV (*entering*) No.

ROB Come on. More than one word.

RAV Absolutely (*Squeaks.*) *Not*. (*Groans.*) Oh . . .

ROB Something really weird has happened overnight, Ravvy. We appear to have pubertised. All in one go.

RAV (*horrified*) You're joking. That thing's supposed to be gradual.

ROB Everything's pointing to it.

RAV *Don't* say that.

ROB Well look at us. You're squeaking like a mouse every few syllables and my hair is dripping grease like a chip factory. And you know how cool my hair was. Combed to perfection. I mean. I know I used to use a bit of gel, but this looks like I stuck my head in a washing-up bowl of it.

RAV And the Neanderthal body-hair. And the stubble! Who's going to fancy *this*?

ROB At least you managed to shave without slashing yourself to pieces. Look at me. Bits of bog roll everywhere. I look like a papier-mâché balloon. And I've been practising for ages as well, getting ready for the big day.

RAV Practising?

ROB You know. With my six-inch ruler as a pretend razor. I'm brilliant with a ruler.

RAV My skin is as tough and rough as a rhino's rear. And Claire is never going to go out with me ever again. It'd be like snogging *sand*paper.

ROB I'm telling you, I was like a gorilla when I woke up this morning. Look. (*Opens a button on his shirt.*) Instant matting. It's everywhere. And my throat's killing me.

RAV It's probably in your throat, too. I'd always thought cut-throat razors referred to shaving on the *out*side, not the inside.

ROB It's really itchy. Maybe grown men body-shave and just wear false body-hair for show.

RAV I doubt it. Though my Uncle Sanjeev does wear a toupee on special occasions to attract the women.

ROB I even had to pluck my eyebrows this morning.

RAV Eh?

ROB (*hurriedly*) In ever such a macho way, mind you. It's just that my eyebrows had grown straight across into one big one. I looked like I should be wrestling a dinosaur or something. I borrowed me mum's tweezers when she wasn't looking.

RAV I wish *I'd* thought of that.

ROB And my feelings. I fancy women twice as much as I ever did – and I didn't think that was possible. The lady across the road from me was doing her windows and my hands started shaking. There was a woman at the bus-stop wearing a mini-skirt this morning and I nearly exploded. I'm a wreck. Not to mention the terrible bouts of wind.

RAV That's not puberty. You've always had that.

ROB Oh. And then there's the dream I had last night.

RAV Eh?

ROB (*clamming up*) Nothing.

Silence.

RAV Well, then there's . . .

ROB (*knowing what he means*) There's . . .

BOTH (*both turn their backs to the audience and look down*) This.

ROB This, strangely, I don't have a problem with.

RAV *Me* neither.

SHELL What are they doing?

LYNZ I can't see. They've got their backs to me.

SHELL Have they noticed us?

LYNZ I don't think so. (*Accidentally knocks her bag onto the floor with a resounding crash.*) Oops.

The boys jump, adjust and turn round.

RAV Who's there?

ROB Girls!

RAV What?

ROB I just thought it was a pile of coats.

RAV Do you think they heard us?

ROB I hope not. Act cool.

RAV Ladies!

ROB All right are we?

SHELL	Fine. What do you want to know for?
ROB	Hostile!
LYNZ	Yes! You don't usually care whether we live or die! (*About to burst into tears.*)
SHELL	Hold onto it, Lynz.
LYNZ	I – !
SHELL	Yes, you can!
LYNZ	But – !
SHELL	Don't think about it!
RAV	Problem?
SHELL	No! We're reading. Now get lost.
ROB	What you reading?
SHELL	(*getting up to them*) What's it to you? Why are you so interested all of a sudden? (*Suddenly aware of Rob's face.*) Whatever happened to your hair?
ROB	My hair? What about your spots?
SHELL	And why have you, Rav, only got one eyebrow straight across your forehead like a caveman?
RAV	Because I didn't think to use me mum's *twee*zers. Oh, man!
LYNZ	What was that squeak? Where did that squeak come from? I hate mice! Don't let it be a mouse! I can't stand any more this morning! Waagh!
SHELL	Lynz, get a grip!
LYNZ	It's too much!
RAV	She's getting hysterical.
SHELL **ROB**	She always does.
ROB	You're probably too hot, Lynz. Take your coat off.

LYNZ   No!

ROB   Let me help you. (*Stretches out hand.*)

LYNZ   You so much as *touch* my coat and I'll – Urgh! What's all that hair on your hand?

RAV   I put glue on my hand and rubbed it along the carpet. What do you think it is, Genius?

LYNZ   You're like a werewolf.

RAV   And you're like an arctic explorer. All you need are the woolly hat and the *gogg*les!

LYNZ   That squeak. It's you!

RAV   So what?

LYNZ   So don't make fun of me, Minnie Mouse!

RAV   *Minn*ie Mouse?

ROB   Okay, lay off Rav. He's had a rough time over the last few hours. Not as rough as Shell, but –

SHELL   And what's *that* supposed to mean?

ROB   Well, your face is a *bit* of a puzzle, isn't it?

SHELL   Puzzle? Oh! As in dot-to-dot! A joke! Did you find it in your mum's make-up bag, Tweezer-Boy?

RAV   That's enough. This is getting us *no*where. The others are going to be pouring in any minute now. We are in a state to say the least and we're going to have to explain it.

SHELL   You're right, Rav. We've got to be mature about this.

ROB   I suppose so. Let's face it. You girls have had the same shock as us. A nasty encounter, but of the female kind. Right, Shell?

SHELL   (*being honest*) I have never seen so many spots in all my life. It's like looking at a pack of dalmations. I feel absolutely gross. If I could get away with wearing a paper-bag over my head with eye-slits in it, I'd do it.

ROB   I feel sweaty and itchy and my hair keeps slithering down my forehead.

RAV   I feel all squashed and hot inside my clothes. My face is sore and I've got a voice like a broken re*cor*der.

LYNZ   Well, at least you haven't got these. (*Opens her coat.*)

RAV   No more, please, Lynz.

ROB   My hands are starting to shake again.

ALL   What are we gonna do?

SAJ   (*entering, absolutely delighted with herself*) Good morning, world! Guess what's happened to me during the night! (*Opens her blazer to reveal her bust.*) Look at these!

LYNZ   Saj! You've got the same as me!

SAJ   And Meg. And Carly. And Joanne. We've all been phoning each other up. Great, isn't it?

LYNZ   Great?

SAJ   Well, I hadn't planned on them so soon, but they're quite nice. Very womanly. And my clothes hang better with them.

SHELL But, the spots!

SAJ   Oh, them. Well, what you gonna do? Wear a paper-bag on your head?

SHELL Don't think it hadn't crossed my mind.

SAJ   That's silly, Shell. A bit of cleansing and eating the right food'll put them straight. We've been reading about it for years in the magazines. We've just got to put it into practice now. Shouldn't take that long. And it doesn't last forever, you know. Anyone done their Maths homework early? I could do with some help before Friday's deadline.

ROB   Well, you're being very philosophical, Saj.

SAJ Thanks.

ROB Why?

SAJ Why not? Been tweezering?

ROB What if I have?

SAJ Good idea. Are you lot coming to Normy's party next Saturday?

RAV Will you stop changing the subject like it's not important, *Saj*! Look at us! *Listen* to us!

SAJ Your voice has broken, Rav. So what? It's not the end of the world. You wait till everybody else arrives. We're all in the same boat. So who's going to make fun of anyone else? No-one. We've all just got to treat each other with a little TLC and a little TCP, that's all.

RAV But I need to –

SAJ Moan your head off. I know. So do we all. But I kinda like these. The other stuff I'll just deal with positively until it passes. Now give me a big hug and get your Maths homework out.

RAV (*hugging her*) What about the scratchy skin?

SAJ Oh, shut up. Come over here and sit down. Claire says to meet her outside the labs at break. Oh, and Shell, Tim is really upset and needs to speak to you. He thinks he's deformed on the one side or something ridiculous. Keeps going on about he'll never bat for England or something. I don't know . . . Lynz, get your coat off and come and sit with us.

SHELL (*delighted*) He asked to speak to me?

Saj and Rav move across the room and sit down. Lynz joins them, taking off her coat.

ROB It's all a bit of an anti-climax really, isn't it?

SHELL She won't even let us moan.

SAJ	(*calling across*) Don't moan. Talk.
SHELL	Eh?
SAJ	Communicate.
SHELL	Oh.

Silence as they think of what to say.

ROB	It's difficult.
SHELL	To just start.
ROB	Yeah.

Silence.

ROB	It's so personal.
SHELL	Yeah.

Silence.

SHELL	I mean, it's not my business really. Boy stuff.
ROB	Girl stuff.
BOTH	Yeah.

Silence.

ROB	Do you wanna hear about the dream I had last night?
SHELL	Yeah!

Innocent

List of Characters

Reno

Finn

Ace

Police Officer

> *Scene: A hospital ward. Ace is unconscious in bed.*
> *Reno and Finn on either side of the bed. There is the*
> *sound of a monitor beeping slowly.*

RENO Some Christmas present.

FINN Who for? You or him?

RENO Don't start that again.

FINN You're selfish. Selfish! All the time, it's you, isn't it?

RENO Yeah, that's right. Me being selfish again.

FINN Even now! Ace is lying here unconscious after the . . . the . . . after what that person did . . .

RENO That person? Who? Who do you mean by 'that person'? Come on, wimp. Spit it out. For once in your feeble life.

FINN And that's *still* all you're thinking about, isn't it? And you didn't give a damn about Trent or Darbo falling off that scaffolding either.

RENO Who do you mean by 'that person', Finn? Me. Say it. I dare you. And I'll give you another slap.

FINN That person who dropped the tablet in Ace's drink! That's who I mean, Reno!

RENO   Not me then. Good. Very wise. 'Cause I wasn't
       involved.

Silence.

FINN   So you keep saying.

Silence.

RENO   I'm sick of justifying myself to you. Everything's
       an accusation. Just like the teachers at school.
       That lot. Everything that went down – I'd
       done it.

FINN   They were right.

RENO   But I didn't like being accused.

FINN   You're mental.

RENO   (*quietly threatening*) Was that another accusation,
       Finn? Because you know what a mess I can make
       of you, don't you?

FINN   Just like at school.

RENO   Just like at school.

FINN   We haven't moved on much since then.

RENO   Speak for yourself, loser. I'm living a great life.
       I've got it made.

Silence.

RENO   This doctor's taking her time. I've got things
       to do.

FINN   Why don't you tell her to hurry up then? Why
       don't you tell her you've got some more deals
       to do?

RENO   Getting brave now, are we? I'm impressed. What
       'deals' would these be?

FINN   Dealing drugs 'deals'.

RENO   Got proof of that, have you?

FINN   It's all right. I'm not a copper. You don't have to
        pretend to me. I know how come you've got that
        stuff. It's because you sell it.

Silence as Reno considers Finn.

RENO   I'll humour you, Sad-Boy. What stuff's that, Finn?

FINN   I know you sell it to kids.

RENO   Really?

FINN   And I know you had some on you tonight.

RENO   Oh?

FINN   And I know you put one in Ace's drink when he
        wasn't looking.

RENO   Do you now? And why would I do that?

FINN   Because Ace didn't want one, so you thought it'd
        be a laugh. Didn't you?

Silence.

FINN   (*yelling*) *Didn't you?*

Silence.

RENO   So what if I did?

FINN   I'd like to kill you.

RENO   You're behind the times, Finn. This is the new
        culture. This is the business of the future. Give it
        time, they'll be legalising this stuff. And I'll be
        right there. One of the new businessmen of the
        twenty-first century.

FINN   Ace is *dying*!

RENO   You're over-reacting. You always over-react.
        He's just having a bad reaction to it. He'll be
        all right.

FINN   He's *dying*! Look at him. Look at the tubes and the monitors. He's on his way out and it's your fault. You're power-mad! You're mental!

RENO   And you're gonna grass me up to the coppers, are you?

FINN   Don't tempt me. I'd like to see you rot for this.

RENO   And you'll be coming down with me, will you? 'Cause I'd tell them everything, you know. About the gang. About you. And how clever you are at organising all those little thefts we do.

FINN   I don't sell drugs.

RENO   No, but you've sold a few tellies and videos that weren't yours though, haven't you?

FINN   I never . . .

RENO   So you're not a saint yourself, are you, Finn? Eh?

FINN   I don't kill people.

RENO   Neither do I. I'm just a businessman. Giving the punters what they want. Just like you and your tellies. And wouldn't your family be proud of you to find out about your business enterprises? Their straight-A student gone bad. And for what? To prove that you were hard. Because it wasn't any fun being the victim, was it, Finn? Fancied wielding a bit of power instead, making a bit of cash and impressing people.

FINN   You've never been a victim . . . You don't know what it's like . . .

RENO   Finn. The great middleman. Shifting stolen tellies to prove he's not a wimp. They'd be so proud, wouldn't they? Wimp.

Silence.

RENO Wouldn't they?

Silence.

RENO So – I'd keep my trap shut if I were you. I don't like people crossing me. And I don't like people saying no to me. Like Ace. And look what's happened to him. Not to mention the others. Trent. Darbo. Bad accident they had, wasn't it?

Finn gets up.

FINN Get all that, did you?

RENO Eh?

Police Officer enters.

POLICE OFFICER Mr Reynolds? Leonard Reynolds?

Reno gets up, alarmed.

FINN (*taking wire out of his sleeve*) Wired for sound.

Ace sits up and pulls the monitor wires off himself.

ACE Just giving the punters what they want.

There is the sound of a monitor flat-lining.

Advent

List of Characters

Deb

Carrie

Danny

Carrie's house. Lounge. Carrie, kneeling on the floor, is staring in wonder at the result of her pregnancy testing kit. Doorbell rings. Carrie jumps. Throws her coat over the kit. Enter Deb.

DEB Why didn't you answer the door?

CARRIE (*absent-mindedly, her mind being on other things*) What? (*Stumbles over to the chair. Sits.*)

DEB Been drinking already? I said, why didn't you answer the door? It's freezing out there.

CARRIE (*distantly*) The door was on the catch, wasn't it?

DEB Yeah. You shouldn't do that. One of these days, someone'll walk in and attack you. Leaving the door on the catch. You're asking for it.

CARRIE (*laughs at irony of this phrase, then coldly, sadly*) Yeah, well. You know me. Always asking for it.

DEB I just said to your mum –

CARRIE (*leaping up*) What? My mum's here?

DEB At our house. I was just talking to her at our house. She's with my mum, remember? They're having a natter and we're off to the party. Your brilliant plan. Them two together, yakking like they do for half the night, our dads off to the match and the boozer afterwards. Then there'd be nobody to see that we didn't sneak off to that party at Jay's house that they didn't want us to go to.

Look. I've brought my mobile so that we can phone them regularly to let them know we're here doing revision when we're at the party really. So, come on then. Danny's meeting us here in a minute. You're not going like that, are you?

CARRIE Look, Deb – I don't really feel like it any more . . .

DEB Eh?

CARRIE I just don't.

DEB But it's all arranged!

CARRIE I just don't . . . I think I'm coming down with something.

DEB Tough. Everyone's gonna be there. And Gareth.

CARRIE (*turning away, very pale*) I don't want to see Gareth.

DEB Oh! You've changed your tune, haven't you? You were all over him last time I saw you. Another one of your brilliant plans. I had to phone your mum a lot that night, too, telling her we were both at Danny's house doing our Technology coursework project so that you could have a date with Gareth, who, let's face it, she hates. Mind you, so do I. I don't know why you don't go out with Danny.

CARRIE Danny's my best friend. We went to junior school together.

DEB So? He still fancies you.

CARRIE (*shocked*) What?

DEB Oh! There I go with my big gob again! I promised Danny I wouldn't tell you, but he's gonna tell you himself tonight anyway, so anyway.

CARRIE (*amazed*) He never said anything before.

DEB Well, I said to him, I said, 'Danny, you're gonna have to say something 'cause she's started fancying Gareth, and he'll treat her crap,' I said. I said, 'Get in there before she makes a fool of herself going out with a moron,' I said, 'Cause she's always liked you the best anyway', I said. Which is true, isn't it?

CARRIE (*quietly*) Yes.

DEB Eh?

CARRIE Yes.

DEB Right. So come on then. You've been really moody lately, getting on my nerves and everything. We planned this party over a month ago. A specially good one for Christmas. You were all for it, so you can't just forget about it now.

CARRIE But, I really feel bad . . . I just don't feel like it . . .

DEB Oh, shut up moaning. (*Looks at her watch.*) Look, forget about getting changed. You'll have to do as you are. Just get your coat on. (*Reaches for Carrie's coat.*)

CARRIE *Leave that alone*!

DEB (*shocked*) What's up with you?

CARRIE Nothing!

DEB You're cracked, you are. I don't see what either of them see in you.

CARRIE Then go to the stinking party and leave me alone, why don't you?

DEB I will!

CARRIE Good!

DEB Tell Danny I'll see him there. (*Just before she leaves.*) Don't bother calling for me tomorrow. (*Exits.*)

CARRIE I won't!

Carrie freezes in the middle of the room, hands to her face. Slowly, tentatively, her hands move down to her abdomen.

DANNY (*singing offstage*) 'Jingle bells, jingle bells, jingle all the way! Oh, what fun it is to ride in a one-horse open sleigh!

Hey!' (*Enters.*) Oy! Did you know your door was on the catch, Brainless?

CARRIE   (*rushing to him, throws arms around him*) Danny!

DANNY   Oh! Merry Christmas to you as well! I didn't even have to get my amusing mistletoe contraption out. Look. (*Puts a really silly mistletoe contraption on his head.*)

Carrie looks at it – then bursts into tears.

DANNY   It's not *that* bad, is it? What's up?

Carrie sits on the floor by her coat.

DANNY   Carrie?

CARRIE   I've always been able to tell you anything, haven't I? Anything at all and you haven't lost your temper with me or gone off or stuff like that. Right?

DANNY   (*concerned*) Well, apart from when you told me you'd arranged a blind date for me and it turned out to be with Sharon Supergob MacKenzie, yeah. I did shout at you for that. But I did forgive you, Ratso, as I *am* an angel. Well, so my Auntie Gladys says.

CARRIE   You've always been such a good friend to me, Danny. My best friend in the entire world . . .

DANNY   Ah, well. Seeing as you've raised the subject, I was going to talk to you about that. I've been thinking, you see. About us and –

CARRIE   Wait a sec, Danny . . .

DANNY   No, no. I've started so I'll finish. I mean I might as well say it now or I'll never say it.

CARRIE   Danny, don't –

DANNY   You see, we've been friends for such a long time and – well, there just isn't anyone I've ever liked as much as you. And I know you're a bit of a rowdy git sometimes, but I know that's all show really. And I'm sure there's others you like, but I'd really like it if we could start seeing each other. Not just as friends. I mean, as a couple, like. You know what I mean? Because I don't know anybody I've ever felt so comfortable with and liked and *trusted* so much as you and –

CARRIE Danny, will you just shut up a minute?

Silence.

DANNY What?

Carrie uncovers the kit.

DANNY (*goes over to the kit, stoops, picks it up*) What's this?

CARRIE A pregnancy testing kit.

DANNY (*as a joke*) What you want one of these for? You're not pregnant, are you?

His face drops as she stares silently at him.

DANNY You're kidding.

Carrie shakes her head at him. Danny takes the mistletoe contraption slowly from his head.

DANNY Maybe this thing is wrong . . .

Carrie takes his hand.

DANNY It's Gareth, is it?

Carrie nods. Danny slowly gets up and walks over to the Christmas tree, Carrie hanging onto his hand until the distance separates them and she can't hold onto him any longer.

CARRIE (*going over to him*) Danny, I . . .

DANNY Get away from me!

CARRIE Danny!

DANNY   What's wrong with you?

CARRIE   It just happened!

DANNY   Where's your *sense*? You stupid, selfish –

CARRIE   It just *happened*!

DANNY   Just happened! Nothing just happens to you. You plan things. You plan everything. Except protection apparently.

CARRIE   I thought he'd have some.

DANNY   Stupid.

Silence.

DANNY   Don't you realise what you've done?

CARRIE   Yes. I've ruined my life. *My* life, Danny. Not yours. So why don't you just push off to the party and let me deal with this on my own? Go on! Go! I don't need you! *Get out*!

Danny looks at her for a moment, hurt, then turns to leave.

CARRIE   (*quietly*) I am so scared, Danny. If you don't stand by me, no-one else will. You've always been my friend.

DANNY   Not as friendly as Gareth, though.

Carrie is silent.

DANNY   Have you been to the doctor yet?

CARRIE   No.

DANNY   Well, you'd better get there, then. Pregnancy's not your only worry.

CARRIE   Was that it? Was that the last stab?

DANNY   Well, don't you realise all the dangers of unprotected sex? Weren't you listening in class? Disease, not just pregnancy.

CARRIE   How is this helping me, Danny? How is your terrifying me helping me?

Silence.

DANNY   This is very difficult for me. You've just changed my life –
in a second. I had these plans for us . . .

CARRIE   I had plans, too! . . . I've always been so clever. So clever
at getting exactly what I want. Planning everything out. I
just didn't see this happening.

DANNY   Well, it did.

CARRIE   I know it did! I'm living every agonising second of it
now! (*Quietly.*) I'm not ready to have a child. I'm fifteen.
I'm still a child myself. I need your help, Danny. I can't
deal with this alone.

DANNY   What about your parents?

CARRIE   I don't even know *how* to start telling them. That my
education's just gone on hold, my future . . . Listen to
me! Me, me, all the time! I'm too selfish to have a child.
But I can't help being that way. And I hate myself for it.
And I hate what I did. And I hate Gareth! So don't walk
out and make me hate you, too!

Silence.

DANNY   Why didn't you tell me before this? Why didn't you tell me?

CARRIE   How could I tell *you* this?

Silence.

DANNY   When are you going to tell your parents?

CARRIE   In the morning.

DANNY   I'll come round. Wait for me.

CARRIE   Thanks.

DANNY   Then there's the local advice clinic to go to. Hopefully,
they'll be able to offer a lot of support.

Danny heads for the door again.

CARRIE   Where you going?

DANNY   Home. (*Turns to her. Throws her a present.*) You might as well have this now. There won't be time for it tomorrow.

CARRIE   (*opening present*) Concert tickets. For tomorrow night.

DANNY   We can't go now. Not with what we'll have to deal with this weekend. Besides – concerts are for carefree kids. And we just grew up. Didn't we?

CARRIE   I don't want to grow up, Danny . . . (*She moves across to him and holds onto him.*)

DANNY   You've got to.

Leper

List of Characters

Ray

A kitchen. Ray is making tea.

RAY   (*filling the kettle*) In Biblical times, lepers were fed. People gave them alms and their own space, standing aside as they passed. It was a form of respect. If I had leprosy instead of HIV, I think I'd have an easier time of it. (*Switches on the kettle.*)

Ray moves across to the work surface and gets a mug off the mug-tree. Proceeds to find the tea, milk, etc., as he speaks.

RAY   HIV. I still don't believe it. I haven't got full-blown AIDS yet. Further down the road . . . Maybe . . . This is just – well, what could you call it? An introduction. I mean, let's look on the bright side. I may not get AIDS . . . I hope. I hope to God. (*Smiles.*) Being ill makes you religious.

The tea-caddy is empty. Ray goes to the cupboard to find a new, cellophane-wrapped box of teabags. Begins wrestling with it.

RAY   I didn't realise until I got it myself how unfriendly the human race can be. How pig ignorant and insensitive. People I thought were my friends haven't phoned me in months. Can they have forgotten my number? That I exist? I doubt it. Now if I had, say, something socially acceptable like – oo – cancer, well! I'd be getting the cards and the commiseration and the sympathy. Perhaps a little fruit-in-a-basket treatment. (*Becoming embittered.*) Not this isolation. This being sent into exile as if I were a stinking criminal! (*Throws spoon, then calms himself.*) I'll have to find that now. (*Smiles.*) Temper, temper. I have to keep a check on it. But,

I'm only human. (*Looks at box.*) And why can I never get the cellophane off these? Why do they seal teabags off so much? Why do I practically need a power-tool to get into them?

Takes scissors gently to the cellophane, removes packaging and puts teabags into caddy.

RAY   The most obvious way tends to be the best solution. Like I say, one of the things I have to contend with is ignorant friends refusing to have anything to do with me now. Excuse me. *Ex*-ignorant friends. And they don't want to see me because they think that I'm gay. One minute you've known them all your life and they're buying you a pint. The next, you're a closet pervert with a master-plan to pervert the entire world. *And* – all together now – it served me *right*. (*Pours boiled water into mug.*)

RAY   Except it didn't. They didn't know what they were talking about. Because they were – and still are, I assume – an ignorant bunch of bigoted morons. I assume this because I don't see them any more.

He chucks the teabag in the bin.

RAY   How can you know someone all your life and still not know them?

He takes a photo out of a drawer.

RAY   I'd known Steph all my life. We went to school together, copied each other's homeworks together, snogged behind the bike-sheds together . . . Ah. Those were the days. We both cried when she went off to university at the other end of the universe. We both had other relationships . . . hot summer flings, cold winter clings . . . But I was never going to marry anyone else. I loved her.

Puts the photo away again.

RAY   Five years after she'd left, we met up again, got married and
      began living in delightfully mortgaged bliss. No kids,
      though. A blessing, now, in hindsight.

Takes tea and sits down with it.

RAY   I had started to feel ill. Frequently. This terrible, perpetual
      'flu I had then turned into wracking bronchitis. So – off
      I went to the doctor – for the eighth time that year. I
      thought she'd just bung me some more antibiotics or
      something. I mean, what she'd given me wasn't touching it,
      but possibly a stronger dosage . . .? But instead, she asked
      me if I had a partner. I said that I had. Married now for eight
      years. Had she a similar infection? Chest infection, maybe?
      I told them, Steph *had* been coughing and hacking on and
      off for ages. I'd no doubt caught the damn thing off her.
      Totally unavoidable. Antibiotics, please? But, no. An
      antibodies test instead.

He puts his mug down and leans forward intently.

RAY   An antibodies test, I had asked. For what? And then the
      lightning bolt struck. For HIV, she'd said. HIV. She explained
      to me, in her dismal office of formica cleanliness, that that
      stood for Human Immunodeficiency Virus – but all I had
      heard was those three, terrible letters. After a while, I started
      to tune in again, through the shock and disbelief, to what
      she was asking me . . . probably, perhaps, maybe, passed on
      to me by . . . Was I monogamous? No other partner but my
      wife? Then if there had been no-one else for eight years,
      I had to face the possibility that *she* had been the one to
      infect me. Infected. By my wife.

He turns the wedding ring on his finger.

RAY   You tell me. Which was worse? That I had HIV? That my wife
      had passed it on to me? Or that she had been with someone
      else? When I got home and confronted her with it, we had

the row of all rows, I can tell you. Look. (*Shows scar on his arm.*) She threw something at me before she left. The scar she left inside was much, much deeper.

He picks up the mug again and drinks.

RAY   (*In response to a question from the audience.*) Sorry? Who had she been with? When? Why? Well, she said she'd been out one night with her mates – you know, a girls' night out – and she'd had too much to drink, lost control and there he was. Whoever he was. The faceless enemy. But now, faced with all these consequences, does it really matter who, where and why it was? What does it mean other than it is all over now. The marriage. Gone. Like that. (*Snaps fingers.*) I cannot live with deceit. She has her demons to face and so do I. Separately.

He finishes the tea and takes the mug to the sink to wash it up.

RAY   And is that the end? Is that it for me now? HIV and drop dead? Not on your life, mate! At the time, I thought it was. After the anger had finally passed, the blaming . . . the rages . . . the quiet torment of missing her . . . the silence of my life . . . things started to pick up.

He turns away from washing up for a moment.

RAY   I know. It surprised me, too. The advice centre I was sent to was brilliant. I mean, I went in there expecting to be measured up for my box, but I was so wrong. I was taken in to see this bloke called Jed, one of the advisors. As I sat in his office of messy paperwork and half-drunk coffee in cheerful coffee-mugs, he gave me what I needed: information and hope. He informed me up to the eyeballs about what I'd got – no resistance to any infection any more – yet what I could do about it. Plenty.

He takes some tablets out and shows the audience.

RAY Here are my tablets, toxic, but used carefully they protect the body as much as they can. I'm lucky I can take them. Steph was taking them and, fortunately, was keeping up with her medication. If she hadn't – if she'd missed three doses in six months – the HIV would have become immune to the tablets. The tablets wouldn't have worked and she would have passed this on to me, meaning they wouldn't have worked for me either. I am, therefore, able to keep the beast at bay. Because that's what it's like to have HIV. It's like having a mad dog living inside me. I have no lead to tie it down with, no protection from it, but if I keep it calm it won't savage me to death. And the way to do that is very simple. If I get unhealthy, my body has no defence against the infection that may develop as a result. So I stay as healthy as possible. I don't drink, I don't smoke, I don't put myself at risk. My diet is highly nutritional and I make sure that I have plenty of sleep. In fact, I live a more healthy life now than I ever did. Ironic, isn't it?

He puts his tablets away.

RAY Will I ever love again? Who knows? I'm still re-structuring my life at the moment. I've made some new friends in addition to the few who *did* stick by me when they found out – some people who accept my HIV condition, but don't condemn me for it. They also can accept that I'm not gay . . . so maybe there's someone else out there for me . . . maybe . . . when I decide to let someone in again. When I trust them. And when I do, she will become part of my stay-safe life. Being sensible. Being protected. Being caring. Until then, I'm okay. I do not live on a grim, wind-swept horizon of fear. I live here – going out to work, having my tea, paying bills, watching television, having a few friends round sometimes, sometimes going out. I do what you do. I live – with care.

He dries up his mug and puts it back on the mug-tree.

RAY   So please don't pity me. And don't consider me to be
      different. I am not a leper. I am not separate from the rest
      of the human race. I'm probably more a part of it than
      most, because I appreciate life. Every second of it. I love
      being here on this planet and I'm going to stay as long as
      I can. And you, my friend, you do the same. Stay safe.
      Understand?

Procedure

List of Characters

Three characters with no names

A   Sir!

B   What's happened?

A   She fell down the stairs.

B   No! Don't touch her! Step back. There's a safety procedure. Did you see what happened?

A   She just tripped and fell.

B   Nobody pushed her? (*Looking around.*) She wasn't in contact with anything?

A   No. Just a clear fall. I think she just wasn't looking where she was going. Is she all right? Shall I get an ambulance?

B   (*squats down by C*) What's her name?

A   Kelly.

B   Kelly? Kelly? Can you hear me?

C   Uhh . . . my head . . .

B   Good. She's awake. (*To C*) Do you know where you are?

C   School.

B   That's right. Do you remember what happened?

A   I told you, Sir. She fell down the stairs.

B   I know. I'm discerning whether she's got any memory loss. (*To C*) Your pulse is good. Where does it hurt, Kelly?

C   At the back of my head.

B   Can you see clearly? Is anything looking blurry?

C   No. It's all okay. Ow!

B There's a nice bump coming up there. Not to worry. (*To A*) Go and get a cold compress.

A Is she all right?

B She's fine. Don't worry. A bump's a good sign. The bleeding's external.

B exits.

C Am I okay?

A Yeah. No blood or fluid from the ears. No tingling in the fingers or toes?

C No.

B And there's no big wires or springs coming out the top of your head, so I'd say there's absolutely no problem at all.

C I've got a bit of a headache.

A I'm sure you have. You've just fallen down the stairs and bumped your head.

B (*running back in*) Here, Sir. Cold compress.

C Urgh! You're supposed to squeeze the cloth out a bit!

A Oh. Soz. Medical Room, sir? Do you want me to take her there?

B Yeah. She can sit there for a while. I'll phone home for you. Is anyone in at the moment?

C My nan.

A I'll tell her what's happened. She can decide if she'd like you to stay at school or not.

C I feel okay.

A Are you sure she doesn't need an ambulance, Sir?

B I'm sure. She's passed the DRABC test.

C What does that stand for?

Fast

List of Characters

Four characters with no names

NOTES:

Why is it important to eat healthily? Why are people attracted to fast food if it isn't as healthy as other food?

A What you got today, then?

B Chicken salad sandwich.

C Wholemeal bread too.

D Very healthy. A good balance of protein, fibre and vitamins.

A And what about you?

B He's having the usual.

C Baked potato stuffed with tuna and sweetcorn.

D Very healthy. Protein, carbohydrates, vitamins, plus essential fish oils which promote healthy skin and lubricate joints.

A It's like eating with a doctor, eating with you.

B The physician should heal himself, though.

C Yeah. What is that slop you're eating?

D Cereal with sliced up fruit, nuts and a good splodge of honey.

A He's eating breakfast!

B Looks terribly gross.

C Like a Waldorf face-pack! Yak!

D Very healthy. And the milk it's slopped up with is an excellent source of calcium.

A What's the bar of chocolate for, then?

B Sugar?

C Iron?

D Pudding. (*To A*) It's about time *you* ate more healthily.

A There's nothing wrong with chips.

B Gravy.

C And a can of pop.

D Very unhealthy.

A I like chips, gravy and a can of pop.

B Fast food.

C Instant gratification.

D All carbohydrate, fat and gas.

A Mind your own business.

B Very fast food.

C You should take off like a rocket with all the CO_2 inside you.

D We have lift-off! What do you eat it for?

A It tastes nice.

B So does ours. But you don't get anything out of yours.

C Apart from spots.

D And wind.

A It's there, it's hot, I grab it. Yum, yum. No waiting.

B You'll be hungry again in five minutes.

C She'll be eating crisps then, I'll bet.

D More carbohydrates. Stuck in a carbohydrate loop, that's your problem.

A Oh, leave me alone.

B Unhealthy and undisciplined.

A Is this a court of law or something? Whatever happened to democracy? I've a right to eat whatever I want.

B A bad eating pattern being established.

D Plus wind. Very uncool. We need shared healthy-eating practices for a healthier life. Slop, anyone?

Relationship

List of Characters

Two characters with no names

NOTES:

Has a friend ever needed to talk? Did you know what to say?

A   Here. Let me help you with that.

B   Thanks.

A   Chucking stuff out?

B   Yeah.

A   What brought this on?

B   I can hardly move around in here. I've got to get rid of stuff.
Everything.

A   Too much. Why are you throwing everything away? Your
diaries? Photo albums? All these clothes?

B   Stuart. I'm throwing Stuart away too.

A   Ah. I see. What happened?

B   He's seeing Zoe.

A   Sit down.

B   Help me with this.

A   Sit down. Please. Throwing your personal possessions away
won't change anything. You're punishing yourself, but you
haven't done anything wrong.

B   I don't know what I did wrong.

A   You did *nothing* wrong.

B   What's wrong with me?

A   Nothing. It's him. He's not going to stay faithful to you or
anybody. He fancies himself too much. He's immature.

B It must be the way I look.

A It's the way you *talk*. Kicking yourself all the time. Are you *listening* to me? Look in this mirror.

B Urgh.

A What do you see?

B Greasy hair. Eyes too far apart. Spots. Your basic Mask Of The Hideous.

A No. That is only what *you* see. Others see differently.

B Like the way my head narrows at the top like a pyramid.

A No. Like your green eyes, your fashionable hair and longest, most aspired-to nails in the class.

B You're just saying that.

A You're just wallowing in self-pity.

B That's unfair.

A It's true. Why did he dump you?

B I dumped him, actually.

A Oh, that's better. A bit of fighting talk! Did he dump you for your looks or your prowess at Mathematics?

B I am now being made fun of.

A Come on. You've got the mirror and the test results to prove it. Which one?

B I am definitely being made fun of.

A Well?

B Neither.

A No kidding. What a shocking conclusion. So you dumped him for what then?

B Because he fancied Zoe.

A And why did he fancy Zoe with the big bottom and the gob to match?

B No taste.

A Immature! He can't deal with your intelligence. He doesn't *want* to deal with your intelligence – particularly as he hasn't got any himself. And he certainly didn't want anyone better looking than himself. I mean, take the attention away from himself? Please!

B But what if it wasn't like that? What if I weren't good at Maths? What if I looked like a gargoyle and smelt like a sewer and he'd *still* gone off with Zoe?

A I'd still like you and I'd still think Stuart was a loser.

B Why?

A Because you're a good, kind, generous person. My friend. I grew up with you. I know you. And I know that Stuart is a low-life punk. Now stop knocking yourself.

B Okay. Fashionable hair?

A Yeah.

B Not too much gel?

A Wouldn't I tell you?

B Yeah. It's good to have a friend.

A I'm your positive reflector. I'll always show you the best in yourself. Just don't do the sewer thing.

B Okay.

Acquaintance

List of Characters

Two characters with no names

NOTES:

Has a friend ever needed to talk? Did you know how to listen?

A What are you doing?

B Chucking stuff out.

A What for?

B Because I want to.

A Don't you want this?

B No. Stuart gave it to me.

A Can I have it?

B Suppose so.

A I've always wanted a bangle like this.

B Don't you want to know about Stuart?

A Who?

B Stuart.

A I know about Stuart. He's gone off with Zoe. After dumping you.

B I dumped him.

A Same difference. Oh. Nice perfume. Can I have some?

B I'm sick of Stuart. I mean, I *was* sick of him. The way he treated me. I – are you *listening* to me?

A Don't shout at me.

B I'm not.

A I came in here to see how you were.

B   No, you didn't.

A   I'll go then.

B   Be like that then.

A   I will.

B   And you can put that bangle back.

A   Here. I don't want it.

B   What are you doing?

A   Leaving.

B   What about being my friend? Listening to me? Don't you want to know what happened with Stuart? What he said? Don't you care?

A   There's something wrong with you. You're tapped.

B   Me?

A   I'm not surprised he went off with Zoe. Sort yourself out, girl. And you could start with your hair. It's a state.

Experience

List of Characters

Two characters with no names

NOTES:

Who are these two characters? What experiences of change do we all have in our lives?

BOTH	We couldn't stay like that forever.
B	I admit, there was no room in there.
A	I mean, at the time I felt comfortable.
B	Yes, it was nice having all that time to walk along on ground level.
A	Twig level.
B	Leaf level – and think how enormous the world was.
A	And how small I was.
B	But it was okay being small.
A	It felt great.
B	No responsibility.
A	Low profile, you see.
B	Very true. Very low.
A	I didn't like the kids picking me up, though.
B	They were always trying to stuff us into jamjars, weren't they?
A	Yeah, but we always got away.
B	Yet I knew it couldn't be like that forever. And that's when I encased myself.
A	It just happened naturally.

B It was just time.

A I don't remember much about it in there.

B Dark, wasn't it?

A I fell asleep.

B There was nothing else to do really.

A Except feel for the changes.

B Dynamic, weren't they?

A To feel my body changing shape like that!

B That tiny body of mine just . . . just pushing out new limbs!

A Wings.

B Antennae.

A Pushing out and folding neatly.

B Waiting.

A Waiting.

B Until it was time.

A And then . . .

B And then . . .

BOTH Whoosh!

A Out we flew!

B I've never experienced anything like it before!

A Not that I didn't like it on the ground . . .

B But airborne? Wow!

A Soaring through the sky!

B Blue and eternal! An atmospheric seascape of space!

A New territory!

B New freedom!

A But even though now I soar . . .

B I won't forget what it was like . . . to touch twig.

Activities

Confidence and Responsibility

Budget

Citizenship

KUIC h)

Speaking and Listening

Y7: 1, 5, 7, 11, 12

Discuss the influence of the media in your group. Look at adverts in 'glossy' magazines, on the internet, television, radio, etc.

- How influenced are we?
- What signs are there of this influence in our lives?
- Are our homes loaded down with unnecessary luxury and fashion items?
- How did you and your family find out about such items before purchasing them?
- What did you think would be added to your life by buying them?
- Do you think your purchase makes you more 'credible' and 'acceptable' to your peer group? Did the advertisement give you this idea? Explain how.
- Are all the messages that advertisements convey true, or are we being seduced into buying via a media fantasy?

Reading

Y7: 1, 2, 3, 4, 5, 14

Are holiday programmes and brochures helpful? Are they informative or deceptive? Is the use of language different between the two? Watch a holiday programme in class, noticing all the text used on screen, then read through some items from a holiday brochure. Bullet-point the differences in two lists, negotiating and deciding upon which points and comments are fair/informative and which are deceptive.

Writing

Y7: 8, 10, 11, 14

Devise a radio script that convinces the listener to buy a totally unnecessary product via persuasive language and an attractive 'must-buy-to-improve-your-life' image! Add sound effects to your script to emphasise the mood of the piece, e.g. the sea, fireworks, etc.

Drama

Y7: 15

Improvise a scene where, three months on, the family in the script have not bought any luxuries. How are they doing? Have they realised that they do need the stuff or do some of them have withdrawal symptoms?

Democracy

Citizenship
KUIC e)

Speaking and Listening

Y7: 1, 2, 5, 10

In pairs, look up the meaning of 'democracy' in the dictionary. Recount an incident, either in your personal life, in school or in the news which you think involved the issue of democracy. Was it an incident which supported democracy or not? Make notes as you talk to each other, then relate your opinions to the rest of the class.

Reading

Y7: 6, 7, 8, 12

How serious are the characters in the text about politics? Close-read the script for evidence in support of your opinion. Bullet-point your findings in a list.

Writing

Y7: 2, 10, 15

Put together a manifesto, a list of five things that you would like to see undertaken in your school, then incorporate these points into a speech you would give in support of your opinions.

You might like to use this structure for your writing:

- Introduce yourself, the name of your party and what you believe in.
- Acknowledge the positive state of your school, yet the need for changes to improve conditions there.
- List the changes which need to be made and the benefit that these changes would bring.
- Sum up the views of your party and why voting for you and your changes would be a good idea.

Drama

Y7: 15, 16, 19

A political party is trying to pass a strange law which will affect schools, e.g. 'All pupils must be bar-coded in place of the usual registration procedure' or, 'For convenience, all food served at school will be replaced by a vitamin-packed and nutritional porridge'. In a group, think of a law and then script a protest rally against it, complete with chanting of protest slogans, key speakers and heckling.

Healing

Citizenship

KUIC g)

Speaking and Listening

Y8: 1, 4, 5, 12

In groups, discuss some of the situations in life which create great emotional responses, e.g. death, divorce, separation, new family members, etc.

Recount some stories about these that you have seen in television drama series and soap operas. Are they accurately dealt with compared to anyone's experience of them in the group?

Using information from the script, the above television drama examples or someone's personal experience, define what you believe to be the emotions connected with each of the situations in life. What stages are involved in dealing with each?

Reading

Y8: 1, 6, 8

In pairs, close-read the text looking at each character's different experience in losing their relative. Look at their different use of language and any underlying meaning attached to what they say. What was it they all ultimately missed about Max?

Writing

Y8: 3, 6, 10

Script a scene between the family five years later, exploring how they have improved and learned to accept what has happened. In what ways have they got on with their lives, though still loving and not forgetting the deceased Max?

Drama

Y8: 13, 14, 15, 16

Improvise in groups the argument about spending between Max and Cara, which she mentions in the script. Two pupils should act the parts, but the remainder of the group should coach the action and responses from a directorial point of view. In so doing, a greater understanding of the relationship between these two characters should then be reached and evaluated by the group. Perform and share your findings with the rest of the class.

Good

Citizenship

KUIC e) and f)

Speaking and Listening

Y7: 1, 7, 12

What would be needed to organise a fund-raising activity in your school? Discuss and bullet-point the main items to be dealt with, then decide the order in which they would have to be carried out. For example, which would need to be organised first: refreshments, ticket sales or teachers to staff the event?

Reading

Y7: 1, 7, 11

What different charities are there in society? Research charity websites on the internet. What needs are there in society today? E.g. awareness and funding for: people with disabilities; the homeless; people experiencing political crises; or natural disasters in other countries.

Writing

Y7: 5, 6, 9

Write about the night of the disco and the success of the venture. What differences between characters are resolved and how? E.g. do Holly and Donna get on better? Is this due to teamwork in solving problems at the disco?

Drama

Y7: 15, 16

Improvise or script in pairs a point before the script's beginning where Ewan and Donna are talking as friends about the disco. Focus on Donna's keenness to get involved due to someone she knows at the hospice. In the script, she is careful to avoid talking about this person in front of everyone. Your improvisation should reveal why.

Suffering

Citizenship

KUIC i) and g)

Speaking and Listening

Y8: 3, 9, 11

What global issues are you aware of via the media at the moment? Through discussion and research with your group, decide which issue to research further and prepare as a formal presentation.

Be aware of your personal contribution to the presentation, then evaluate this as part of an overall final evaluation after the presentation has been given.

- What research did you do?
- Was the research effective, or could you have picked up on certain key points?
- Could your liaison with others in the group have been improved upon? Did you take into consideration the research others had done, and positively develop it with your own input?
- Were the visual aids you produced appropriate?
- Was your final conclusion effective enough to convey its message to the class?

Reading

Y8: 1, 2, 5, 11

Find out about Fairtrade, following up on points made in the script.

- What is the overall aim of Fairtrade?
- In what way do you think it has an interest in 'the human factor' of business?
- What is the problem faced by farmers in such places as Chiapas, Mexico?
- How does Fairtrade try to support the needs of these farmers?

- What is your own awareness of Fairtrade? What products do you know of that have been supported by this organisation?
- What is your opinion of Fairtrade?

Writing

Y8: 5, 7, 13

Write a letter to Azzy from his father, trying to explain about the nature of the divorce. It is important that your letter should also have the sensitive tone of the parent trying to convey the fact that he still loves Azzy, regardless of the divorce.

OR: Y8: 5, 7, 13

Write a thank-you letter from Azzy to Rod in appreciation of his understanding and compassion at a time when it was greatly appreciated.

Drama

Y8: 14, 15

Using your research, improvise or script a piece spotlighting a farmer and a person from Fairtrade, showing how this business relationship has improved both of their lives.

Business

Citizenship

KUIC a)

Speaking and Listening

Y8: 12

In a group, try to establish the nature of the business transaction that occurs in this script. Argue positively from Deel's point of view, then from that of Slater, listing the points you make in support of their intentions.

Now go through the process again, but highlighting the negative outcome of their intentions.

Use this information to discuss the nature of business for those who seek to be corrupt within it. What is it that they want? What part of their own nature do they motivate themselves with in order to get what they want? What is your opinion of this with regard to human rights, specifically the rights of those unwittingly being manipulated by the business-making of others?

Reading

Y8: 5, 7, 10

In pairs, through close reading of the language, trace the element of corruption in the script, not only in what the characters do and say, but also through what can be inferred about them as people.

Writing

Y8: 5, 13

You are Slater. Write a statement from him, trying to persuade readers that his way of doing business is acceptable.

Drama

Y8: 14, 15, 16

Improvise a protest at the warehouse by its workers with regard to its closing. There should be spotlights within the piece by workers expressing their personal circumstances and the financial difficulties they are experiencing.

Fantasy

Citizenship

KUIC a) and h)

Speaking and Listening

Y9: 1, 5, 7, 8

How do you see yourself in ten years' time? Doing what? Based on which of your personal skills? Based on what decisions and choices?

Within your group, discuss these points, planning out the route which each person in your group would need to take to get there – people to see, exams to take, letters to write, research to do, interview techniques to study, etc.

To conclude: was anyone previously aware of all the planning that needed to be done? The group should share its opinions with regard to what they have realised in going through this process.

Reading

Y9: 1, 10

In pairs, trace and list the language of living in denial in the script. What conclusions can you come to about these teenagers and the reality of their thinking? Why are they so sure of themselves and yet so completely wrong?

Writing

Y9: 5, 13

Write a statement from yourself ten years into the future. What are you doing in life? What advantages do you have because you worked hard to get what you wanted? Be realistic yet positive in your statement, describing how you strove for the possible and the best that you could get.

Please note: Being realistic does not mean limiting yourself to certain choices. It means searching down every avenue available to you. The reality is that there is a lot more on offer to you if you just know where to look – and that is why you need to plan and research your future.

Drama

Y9: 14, 15, 16

Using the script as a basic structure, but without the Careers Officer, script a conversation between the three teenagers which is much more positive and realistic with regard to the kinds of career they desire.

Relationships and Respect

Empathy

Citizenship

KUIC a) and l)

Speaking and Listening

Y8: 1, 3, 4, 5, 8, 10

If you lived in another part of the world, how different would life be for you?

In pairs, research a different community, then report back to the group, giving clear explanations and using any charts, diagrams or pictures available on issues such as housing, educational facilities, work available, transport used, etc.

Reading

Y8: 1, 2, 4, 7

In pairs, research a community currently in need of support for some reason. From the evidence that you find, highlight and make notes of their needs and the reasons for the community's dilemma.

Using an image or diagram as a focus, present your information as part of a display board of other information with the rest of the group's findings.

Read each other's findings and look for common links between all these different communities to recognise the issue of 'the global community'. For example, problem areas such as climate and political upheaval should be linked, but also positive 'kinship links', such as similar educational systems, sports, etc.

Writing

Y8: 3, 9

Based on your earlier research, imagine that you live in a different country that has an alternative culture to your own. Describe the place in which you live, the education received, what you eat and drink, where you go to socialise with others, and some of the natural or political problems that have to be dealt with.

Drama

Y8: 14

Improvise the meeting of Jon and Marie. Under what circumstances might they meet? Your improvisation should convey the empathy these two characters have for each other as well as details about their lives taken from the script.

Help

Citizenship

KUIC b) and g)

Speaking and Listening

Y7: 1, 4, 5, 7, 12

Discuss the issue of prejudice within your group. How many different kinds of prejudice are evident in school, including prejudice based on gender? How are human rights infringed upon as a result? Negotiate and decide upon ways in which pupils' human rights can be protected and supported within the school.

Reading

Y7: 1, 2, 6, 8, 12

If prejudice is based on fear of what is the victim fearful? In pairs, search for words based on this in the text.

Writing

Y7: 3, 5, 9

Script another version of this story based around a different form of prejudice. It should involve more positive characters, both of whom are able to resolve their conflict by the end of the piece.

Drama

Y7: 15, 18

Workshop the idea of prejudice as an expression of the need of someone to have power over another person, based on the fact that they feel inadequate and powerless themselves.

- Get into pairs. Label each other A and B.
- A has two minutes to talk down to B and make them do anything they want to – within reason!
- Now swap over, putting B in the power-seat for two minutes.
- Share your feelings with the group. What did it feel like to have that kind of power and what were the different feelings of being a victim?
- Repeat the process now, but adding an element of picking on the victim for the colour of their eyes and, in the swap-over, for the fact that they are/aren't wearing a watch.
- Discuss: are the feelings the same as they were before? Did the eye-colour/watch-wearing discrimination change these feelings? Is the language of prejudice meaningless? Is it just people desiring power over others? How, then, do we deal with it?

Caring

Citizenship

KUIC a) and c)

Speaking and Listening

Y7: 1, 4, 5, 12

Discuss in your group which character dealt with the caring situation best.

To assist with your discussion, make a chart of all the names of the family members, then bullet-point underneath each name how they were able to support Matt. In conclusion, is caring a whole-family commitment? Why?

In the same way, if it were a group of people that needed support, would that make it a community commitment?

Reading

Y7: 6, 7, 8

In pairs, trace how emotional stress builds through the language of the family members. Is there any evidence, in the things the characters say and do, that points to where the stress is coming from specifically?

Writing

Y7: 2, 10, 11, 13, 15

Design a leaflet about the importance of 'care in the community', but not in the usual meaning of the expression.

It should cover the general idea of caring:

- Care of relatives with poor health.
- Caring we show to people at school.
- Showing our families that we care at home.
- Caring for your own needs – exercise, sleep, a nutritional diet, self-esteem.

Consider the level of language and layout for a Year 6 audience.

Drama

Y7: 17, 18, 19

Plan an improvisation with a partner based on a caring situation, e.g., a child looking after an elderly relative. Research correct medical terms, the names of organisations, etc., for use in the piece.

Keep a reflective record of how your drama developed to share with the rest of the group in an evaluation session.

Marriage

Citizenship

KUIC a) and g)

Speaking and Listening

Y8: 5, 6, 11

What reasons do you think people have for opting either for marriage or a partnership without marriage?

Initially basing your discussion on the script, create two spider diagrams for Helen and Jack exploring firstly why Helen wants to marry, and secondly why Jack would rather she lived with James.

Through further discussion, try to think of other reasons why people opt for marriage or not, then add them to the charts.

What conclusions can you draw about marriage?

Pick up on this discussion after researching the facts and figures of marriage and talking to people who are married or living with a partner. What conclusions can you come to now? Is marriage a tradition or, as with Helen, an emotional need, or is it something else?

Reading

Y8: 1, 2, 3

Using texts, the internet, etc., research any statistics you can find on marriage, different religious ceremonies and how marriage is carried out in various global communities. Follow the links on the Heinemann website for UK statistics.

Writing

Y8: 5, 8, 10

Write a diary entry or letter to a friend from James, describing the difficulties being faced with Jack.

Drama

Y8: 15

Work with a partner on an improvised scene between Jack and James in which a positive outcome is achieved.

Mob

Citizenship

KUIC a) and h)

Speaking and Listening

Y8: 2, 11

Recount to each other in your group stories of being bullied. 'The Mob' in school is the gang of bullies. How did you deal with the situations you were all caught up in? Could more be done in school to support you?

Make a chart to aid discussion of who 'The Mob' could be in the outside world. The script is based on a real event. The *News Of The World* published a list of known paedophiles and groups of people took it upon themselves to seek out some of these alleged paedophiles, and others they suspected. The mobs stoned their houses and attacked them. One reported case was of the house of a paediatrician being stoned by mistake. Are there other examples of 'The Mob'? What or who motivates them to their acts of violence?

Reading

Y8: 1, 2, 3, 6, 10

Research with a partner and make notes on examples in the press of mob violence. List five stories and focus on the key idea of what motivated their need to attack.

How did the style of each article present 'The Mob'? Was there an element of emotional language leading to bias? Should the press do this, or just relate the facts? Give reasons for your opinion.

OR: Y8: 1, 2, 3, 15

Research Roman times when Shakespeare's *Julius Caesar* was set. What evidence of mob violence was there then? How much was stirred up, as with Mark Antony, by the government or the emperor?

Writing

Y8: 10, 12, 13, 16

Write two newspaper articles about the same story – an act of mob violence. One should be a straightforward relating of the facts, but the other should be more biased in its style, revealing very strong anti-mob sentiments to the reader.

Your articles should contain:

- A description of the crime committed.
- The time, date and place of the incident.
- Statements from those involved and witnesses.
- How the police dealt with the incident.
- Any future court dates or measures to be taken (usually found in the final paragraph).

Drama

Y8: 13, 14, 16

With your group, collaborate on your own improvisation based on mob violence, using the techniques of spotlighting and thought tracking to reveal what you think is going on in the minds of the mob and its victim.

After performing the piece, share your own ideas of the effectiveness of the piece and what you hoped for, before the audience give their opinions. How do the two sets of opinions compare?

Bond

Citizenship

KUIC a)

Speaking and Listening

Y9: 7, 8, 9

Discuss whether the new areas science is investigating (e.g. cloning, foetal-tissue experimentation in the treatment of Parkinson's disease) are going to be beneficial and supportive of life/the quality of life, or, in the long term, detrimental and divisive/harmful to society. Share your group opinions with the rest of the class.

Reading

Y9: 1, 2, 4, 7

Trace the plight of women in a range of communities. What lies at the base of this prejudice? To what extent does persecuting and denying basic rights to such women undermine human rights and corrupt the basic stability of relationships, the family, the workplace and society itself?

Writing

Y9: 2, 5, 9

Write a continuation of the story, scripted or in prose, as two officials talk afterwards about the wishes of the woman wanting her own baby. Their reactions and opinions should be based on the script. Opposing views might be shown – the hardliner as opposed to the other more conscience-ridden person, not sure whether the present state of the nation is akin to 'Utopia'.

Drama

Y9: 14, 15

Imagine a future world in which some other area of human rights is being abused. Improvise a protest scene outside government headquarters.

Once performed, evaluate whether it was effective by talking to the audience you performed it in front of – a small group. Adjust accordingly, then perform it to them again. Do they consider it to be more effective this time? Why?

Healthy, Safer Lifestyles

Travel

Citizenship

KUIC: a) and i)

Speaking and Listening

Y7: 1, 2, 5, 6, 7, 13

In your group discuss another area in which there is a risk factor to be prepared for, and dealt with, carefully.

What risks would there be? What precautions would need to be taken and what preparations made? What eventualities might there be if no precautions are taken?

Reading

Y7: 1, 2, 4, 6, 10, 13

After looking at some travel websites, travel brochures and other appropriate sources of information, select five different destinations around the world and find out/determine the different precautions and preparations which would need to be taken before travelling there.

Writing

Y9: 2, 10, 11, 18

Put together an advice sheet for a Year 7 readership about the risk assessment needs of either:

a)   preparations before travelling to some destination, or

b)   a particular event that needs planning.

Drama

Y7: 15, 16

Improvise or script the scene in which the family have just returned from their holiday. How did they cope with what they chose to take with them?

Smoke-Screen

Citizenship

KUIC: a) and f)

Speaking and Listening

Y7: 1, 4, 11, 13, 19

What does your group know about smoking? Are you aware of any statistics or laws about the subject? What is public opinion like on the subject? What are your school rules on smoking? Why do people smoke? What are the consequences of smoking? Are there any helplines for people who want to stop smoking?

Structure a plan within your group to investigate these areas and agree on a completion date for all information to be brought back to the group for evaluation. Your plan should include organising tasks, setting up interviews, etc.

Findings should be related to the rest of the class in the form of a group presentation.

Reading

Y7: 7, 10

Reading through the information for the Speaking and Listening activity above, make preparations and shape the material to produce a school information booklet which is against smoking.

Writing

Y7: 10, 11, 13

Write the school information book which is against smoking based on the previous activities.

Drama

Y7: 16, 17, 18

Write and perform the script that your group thinks the pupils in Smoke-Screen would finally have performed.

Pressure

Citizenship

KUIC a) and g)

Speaking and Listening

Y7: 1, 2, 5, 7, 12

Discuss peer-group pressure:

- Why do negative groups of people form in the first place? What do they all hope to get from being together?
- Why is there so much pressure on pupils to belong to one 'friendship' group or another?
- What emotions are underneath all this belonging to a group, sticking together and 'being one of us'?
- Do you think it is the same in the adult world? Does anyone in your group have a story to tell of this?

In what ways could people's behaviour change so that there would not be so much negative pressure on others to belong to their group or face the consequences?

Reading

Y7: 1, 2, 7, 10, 11

Collect newspaper articles about children and teenagers who have succeeded in something recently, e.g. people who have put together a presentation in school or some other venue, have been involved in a sporting or charity-based activity, or have won a competition.

Read about them. Have they been under some pressure to achieve what they wanted? In what way was it a different kind of pressure from one which threatens wellbeing – as negative peer-group pressure does?

Writing

Y7: 9, 10, 11, 12, 13

Write about someone you know, or have read about, who has achieved something in their lives, however small it may seem. What help did they receive from others to get what they wanted? Explain how the pressure was positively motivated and, therefore, had a positive outcome.

Drama

Y7: 15

Improvise a scene where Ingram and Naylor confront Knox after Ingram has been a great success in the school production.

OR: Y7: 15

Improvise a scene where Ingram goes to talk to the people at Turnstiles about her personal concerns.

Gross!

Citizenship

KUIC g)

Speaking and Listening

Y8: 1, 5, 11

How knowledgeable are you about growing up?

After discussion with your group, list the kind of knowledge school provides, then make a separate list of what you have learned from the media, friends, etc. Decide on what else you need to know about that is not being dealt with enough, e.g. are physical signs of growing up being dealt with, but not the emotional needs of teenagers?

Reading

Y8: 2, 4, 5, 7

Beginning in a group set-up, list the main problems that teenagers cope with, both physical and emotional.

Next, read through teenage magazine problem pages on your own, listing the problems that crop up most. Share your findings with a partner and compare your research. Return to the group and evaluate all your findings. Are the findings what were expected? How realistic are the problems in the magazines with regard to the everyday needs of the teenager? Did reading teenage magazines on a regular basis influence anyone's original choices?

Are our real needs very basic and not as complex as magazines would make them seem?

Close-read the problems of the teenagers in the script. Sweeping aside all the complexity of their speech, what underlying problems does each teenager have and how could it best and most simply be dealt with? E.g. wanting to be liked.

Writing

Y8: 7, 9, 10

Write a diary entry for one of the characters in the script in which they are dealing with their problems positively.

Drama

Y8: 15

Improvise a family scene where a teenager is helped to deal positively with a difficult emotional crisis for them, e.g. being stood up on a date.

Innocent

Citizenship

KUIC a)

Speaking and Listening

Y9: 5, 7, 8

Using the proverb 'Money is the root of all evil', discuss within your group whether this is true within the script, or whether other issues also arise.

Reading

Y9: 1, 4, 7

In pairs, using local newspapers, identify types of crime being committed in the local community. What assistance is given to victims in these cases by police, local authorities, etc.? Could more be done?

Bullet-point suggestions you would make in a letter intended for the local authority to prevent such crimes from happening in the first place.

Writing

Y9: 2, 13

Imagine you are the prosecuting counsel in a court case following the main action of the script. Write your opening statement to the court, persuasively explaining why this man should be found guilty of his crimes and punished accordingly. Refer to evidence in the text.

Suggested structure:

- Introduction stating who the man is and the crime of which he is being accused. What you intend to prove to the court as to the reason he committed the crime.
- Briefly what you believe to be his motivation for doing what he did.
- The harm caused to his fellow citizens by this man's approach to life.
- Concluding statement stating the responsibility of the jury in making sure that he gets a fitting punishment.

Drama

Y9: 14

Improvise the scene which reveals how and why Ace and Finn decided to set up Reno.

Advent

Citizenship

a), f) and g)

Speaking and Listening

Y9: 8, 9, 10

Divide the discussion group into two advice groups, one to counsel Carrie and the other to counsel Danny. Both are suffering. What advice would you give them? What advice would you have given them that could have made Carrie and Danny choose different paths before Carrie went with Gareth in the first place?

Swap tasks, then pool your opinions. How does the advice differ between the two groups?

Reading

Y9: 1, 2, 4

Read through the scene between Carrie and Deb. What kind of a friendship do they have? Does the evidence you find explain why Deb is so quick to leave Carrie when she loses her temper?

How should Deb have reacted instead?

Writing

Y9: 2

Write the scene that could have taken place between Deb and Carrie, had their friendship been more positive and caring, where Deb advises Carrie about the dangers of her irresponsible behaviour and actually talks her out of going with Gareth, hence avoiding the pregnancy crisis.

Drama

Y9: 12, 14

Put the three characters of Deb, Carrie and Danny into spotlights to express in an improvisation how they feel about their predicaments at the moment. Don't forget, Deb does not know that Carrie is pregnant, so will be explaining how she feels about Carrie and herself having had a row, wondering whatever is the matter with her. Particularly focus on the regret that both Danny and Carrie feel – Danny for not intervening in Carrie's foolish interest in Gareth before, and Carrie for being so single-minded and unthinking with regard to the consequences of her actions.

Leper

Citizenship

KUIC a), c), f) and g)

Speaking and Listening:

Y9: 1, 7, 9

How much do you know about HIV through PSHE? What do you find out about it in the script? What else do you need to know, in your opinion, to become well-informed? Discuss these points and list ideas within your group.

Why do you think it is that, even after extensive coverage in the 1980s and 1990s, there is still a terrible ignorance with regard to HIV? What does this reveal about human nature? What, in the considered view of your group, is a good way of keeping the issue in the minds of the public so that it is constantly addressed?

Reading

Y9: 6

Trace how the character of Ray is conveyed as an emotionally strong person dealing with an extraordinary situation, even though he has understandable moments of weakness. Use quotations to support this image of him.

Why, in your opinion, do you think the choice was made to deal with the subject matter in this way rather than any other?

Writing

Y9: 13

Having carried out some prior research on the effects of HIV across the world, write an emotional statement persuading the government to take more action to deal with this crisis – perhaps a special congress being set up to establish some major political action to prevent further spread of the disease and re-educate people.

Drama

Y9: 14

Work in a group of three to shape an improvisation for one of you to act as Steph, relating her side of the story. What made her knowingly pass HIV on to Ray?

This is a complicated issue to deal with. Painting Steph as the total villain of the piece would not be a productive exercise. She is an emotionally complex character who ultimately did a terrible thing. Was it an act of denial about her own condition? An act of hatred? If the latter, how had their relationship, which had been so loving, turned into something so terrifyingly dark?

Your improvisation should show how corrupt human nature can become, the path that led to it, but also *the alternative choices that we all can make* to support instead of destroy the citizens of this world.

Macbeth on the Loose

By Robert Walker

Grantham High School is staging
Macbeth. But as rehearsals
proceed, intrigue among the cast
takes on Shakespearean
proportions . . .

Robert Walker enables students to gain
an understanding of the plot, language,
themes and main characters of *Macbeth*
in the context of a highly accessible – and
witty – original play!

Accompanying activities provide
invaluable links to the Framework for
Teaching English.

Age 10+ ISBN 0435 23333 5